'NEW SAVOURY RECIPES

from a Farmhouse Kitchen
on the
Isle of Bute
Scotland

Written, designed and published in Scotland by
CAROLE HOWARD
'New Farm'
Mount Stuart
Isle of Bute
Scotland

'NEW FARM' SAVOURY RECIPES

Written, designed and published in Scotland by
CAROLE HOWARD
'New Farm'
Mount Stuart
Isle of Bute
Scotland
Tel: 01700 831 646
Fax: 01700 831 646
e-mail: newfarm@isleofbute.freeserve.co.uk
web site: http://www.isle-of-bute.com/newfarm

Illustrated by
JESSICA HERRIOT
Balmory Cottage
Ascog
Isle of Bute
Scotland
Tel: 01700 502 725

Edited by
JOAN WALTERS
Woodend House
Loch Fad
Isle of Bute
Scotland
Tel: 01700 505 619

Printed and bound by
GARDNER GIBSON (PRINT) LTD
5 Neil Street
Renfrew
Scotland
Tel: 0141 886 2258
Fax: 0141 885 0951

Copyright©Carole Howard 1999

This book is dedicated to

Eric Miller
(1929-1999)

a much missed, kind and gentle man.

'NEW FARM' SAVOURY RECIPES

All credit is due:

To my Editor, **JOAN WALTERS**, who has not only edited this book but she has typed it, helped design it, <u>and</u> made gallons of coffee! She's also laughed and cried along with me in the process.

To my Illustrator, **JESSICA HERRIOT**, thank you for your beautiful illustrations, not only throughout this book but also for the artwork which adorns the walls of my home.

To my Mother, **MAUREEN FENBY**, who initially inspired me to cook. She is a talented cook herself, and even as a great grandmother she still feeds 150 farmers at a twice-weekly cattle market in Yorkshire.

To my Husband, **MICHAEL**, who has had to cook many of his own meals whilst I've been busy writing this book.

To my Children, **MICHAELLA**, **VICTORIA** and **STUART** thank you for your patience. Now this book is finished we should be able to get back to our routine.

To all my **GUESTS**, thank you for coming, and thank you for coming back time and time again.

To all of you…… a huge, big **THANK YOU!**

'NEW FARM' SAVOURY RECIPES

INTRODUCTION

"There is absolutely no way on earth we are moving to a remote Scottish Island in the Inner Hebrides," said Michael my husband.

Three weeks later we moved. Our transit van was full to the gunnels with all our worldly goods. It took us over 16 hours to travel the 550 miles from our home in Somerset, a 7-bedroom cluttered, rambling old farmhouse to our new home, a 300 acre farm with a 2-bedroom farmhouse on the Isle of Gigha. We had sold almost everything we owned to realise enough capital to become tenant farmers as opposed to managing farms for others as we had done for the last 10 years.

Our friends in Somerset bid us a fond farewell and, with them thinking we were totally mad, we set off up the road to pastures new. We were both seasick on the ferry and the wild, wet and windy weather that greeted us in November on the Island of Gigha was not very welcoming. However, Gigha is a lovely island, situated just off the Kintyre peninsula in Argyll, Scotland. This small strip of land, 7 miles long and $1\frac{1}{2}$ miles wide at its widest point, is home to 120 people.

We altered the house so that we could accommodate our first ever bed and breakfast guests. We had only one room available to let and no central heating. The guests had to eat with us in the kitchen huddled around the AGA. They seemed to enjoy it and so did I.

We soon outgrew the farm and the house. Within 5 years we had accumulated 80 cows, 300 sheep, 20 beef cattle, a few hens, a dog and 2 children. We were bulging at the seams! So we started to look for another farm. **'New Farm'** was the first and only that we viewed. It was situated on another island the beautiful **Isle of Bute**. As the crow flies it's only 40 miles from the Isle of Gigha but over 100 miles by road or 60 miles if we took 3 ferries!

'**New Farm**' was almost 3 times bigger at over 1,080 acres with a house that was once 4 cottages. We were very fortunate to be offered the tenancy on the Bute Estate from the Marquess of Bute. Apart from being desperately under capitalised we realised that the take-over date for the **Isle of Bute** farm was 6 months earlier than the hand-over date for the Isle of Gigha farm. So we farmed on two islands for 6 months. It was fun to say the least!

Michael concentrated on building a brand new dairy unit for the cows to move into. I spent my time trying to stretch our few sticks of furniture from the 2-bedroom farmhouse on Gigha to what was now a 6 bedroom farmhouse on Bute. We knocked the cottages into one 'L'-shaped house with a 'guest end' and an 'our end', separated by the farmhouse kitchen. Stuart our third child was born 2 weeks after we moved in and we took our first bed and breakfast guests a week later, just after the cows arrived from Gigha. Life was certainly hectic!

I had decided that because of our lack of cash to spend on what Michael refers to as luxuries i.e. furniture, I would design the house with a very minimalist feel to it. (I had done the cluttered look in Somerset.) I chose lots of muslin and very light colours mostly white, cream and pale sage green. Typically for an estate house the walls were covered in woodchip wallpaper. We stripped it all off and replaced it with plain lining paper. We then painted the walls with the palest sage green that I could find.

I had by then met a talented local artist called Jessica Herriot. Within a couple of weeks she totally transformed the blank green walls, using them as a large canvas for her 'freehand' artwork. She took her inspiration from our overgrown garden of wild flowers. Soon the walls were growing with wild dog roses, brambles, crab apples, vetch and honeysuckle. It is beautiful and I love it and so it seems do the guests. Jessica has a very light hand (as you will see from the illustrations in this book) and teamed with the minimalist furniture and pale fabrics the house is a wonderful calm place to relax and unwind.

We are 6 miles from the nearest town of Rothesay and shortly after taking our first guests at **'New Farm'** I realised that I might have to cook their dinner! It wasn't long after I started offering evening meals that a resident guest asked if some of their friends who lived on the island could join them for dinner. These local guests enjoyed their meal and asked if they could come back another night with some of their friends... and, as the saying goes, the rest is history. We now do bed and breakfast, morning coffee, lunches, afternoon teas and dinners. We have a few coach parties every year and we also cater for special occasions such as weddings and anniversaries. To say that it has got out of hand would be an understatement!

I couldn't manage to run this ever-expanding business and raise 3 very young children without help, so when Lorna Stirling joined us as the children's nanny she was like manna from heaven. Lorna was with us for nearly 4 years. Sadly she has left us now to work in a local nursery but it is thanks and all credit to Lorna that our children, Michaella 7, Victoria 6 and Stuart rising 5, are to a certain extent reasonably user-friendly and mostly well behaved. We all love living at **'New Farm'** and I hope our guests feel the same even if they are only with us for a short while.

Right from the very start I decided that I did not want to run a normal restaurant offering a menu, cooking the same food day after day. What I wanted was farmhouse lunch and dinner parties reminiscent of threshing days with everyone all around one table. So when guests ring to book I promise not to serve them anything they are allergic to or prefer not to eat. I also do not have (or want to have) a license to sell alcohol so guests bring their own wine, or in some cases their own bar!!! Most lunchtimes and evenings the party is in full swing with good music, farmhouse style food, and guests enjoying themselves at one big communal table. In this way strangers meet and make friends and hopefully everyone has a good time.

Almost all the food I serve is grown on our own farm and my ethos is **"If we cannot grow it, make it or rear it then I will source it locally on our island the beautiful Island of Bute"**. (Needless to say you may find the odd banana and citrus fruit that may owe its existence to parentage abroad!)

The garden is now a little more tamed and we grow most of our veg and all our own herbs. We make our own bread and preserves, we rear all our own beef, lamb and pork and our free-range hens oblige us with a never-ending supply of eggs. Our near neighbours Ninian and Rhona McAlister at Bruchag Farm produce the highest quality double cream, which is delivered fresh every day. The Isle of Bute Creamery supplies mature cheddar cheese. All my smoked fish (trout, salmon and haddock) comes from Ritchies of Rothesay who also provide an excellent mail order service. I have never had much success growing fruit and I am always eternally grateful to all the local people who turn up with surplus home-grown produce. One dear friend who loves fishing on Loch Fad, the largest loch on the island, keeps me supplied with fresh trout, and local sea fishermen bring the fruits of the sea to my kitchen door.

'New Farm Bed & Breakfast & Restaurant' is not just a
'Taste of Scotland' establishment but is now more a
'Taste of "New Farm" & the beautiful Island of Bute'.

This book has been written at the insistence of my guests. It has been an interesting experience bringing it all together, mainly because there has been a certain amount of reluctance on my part to put pen to paper. But it is written now and I hope you enjoy reading it and cooking from it...!

(By the way, if and when you find any mistakes please let me know. My telephone number is printed at the front of this book.)

'NEW FARM'
FOOD APPLIANCES

Cooker: Throughout this book I have been deliberately vague about cooking times as everyone's cooker behaves differently. My cooker, which is a 56-year-old AGA (fondly referred to as 'Bessy') is extremely temperamental and very moody. Depending on which way the wind is blowing bread can take anything from 25 to 70 minutes to bake. I suppose I'm used to her ways and all of her moods and every so often I forgive her because she does keep my kitchen warm and welcoming! For those of you with better behaved gas or electric cookers, I have included oven temps and times but please use your own judgement as to whether a dish is cooked to a tee or burnt to a crisp!

Food Mixer: I have a 15-year-old 'Kenwood' that, like my AGA I am very attached to but unlike 'Bessy' the AGA it doesn't have a name. Unfortunately its working life is nearly at an end but I can't complain. I think I have more than had my money's worth! The replacement will more than likely be the same make but will be a more up to date model.

Food Processor: A couple of years ago I treated myself to the largest domestic size food processor that I could find. It was at the time wildly extravagant but I have never had any regrets. It is totally invaluable for shredding, grating and slicing. For me the capacity of the bowl was the most important consideration when buying this machine. Up until now I have shied away from buying the larger commercial appliances because I want my kitchen to be homely and welcoming and not all stainless steel and clinical.

Hand-held Blender: When I was given one of these things for Christmas it lay lonely and unused in a kitchen drawer until Easter! One day when my liquidizer died the blender was rescued from its lonely existence in the kitchen drawer. These days I find it is an absolute godsend. It is just a marvel for quickly blending soups to leave a 'bite' or whizzing up some maple cream.

Microwave Oven: Yes, I do own a microwave oven! I use it mostly for hasty defrosting and last minute sauces. It has none of the fancy buttons, switches or pre-set timings of today's trendy models. It is 17 years old and has an 'on' and an 'off' button and that is all!

'NEW FARM' SAVOURY RECIPES

CONTENTS

INTRODUCTION	page 5
SOUPS & BROTHS	page 12
SALADS	page 24
VEGETABLES	page 34
MEATY MAIN COURSES	page 46
VEGGIE, VEGAN & FISH	page 58
BACK TO BASICS	page 68
A WEE TASTE BUD TICKLER!	page 78
INDEX	page 84

'NEW FARM' SAVOURY RECIPES

I MAKE NO PRETENCE AT ALL THAT

THIS COLLECTION OF RECIPES

OFFERS ANYTHING APPROACHING

A BALANCED DIET.

'NEW FARM' FOOD IS TO BE

EATEN, SAVOURED AND ENJOYED.

THESE ARE THE RECIPES THAT I COOK

IN MY FARMHOUSE KITCHEN

AND I'M OVERWEIGHT......!

EAT, SAVOUR & ENJOY
(& EXERCISE LATER...!)

'NEW FARM' SOUPS & BROTHS

The basic principles for making farmhouse soups and broths are all very much the same:

1. Sweat your onion(s) in butter and a wee drop of cold water. (The water stops the onions colouring.)
2. Add the prepped vegetables and any herbs.
3. Cover with a good quality stock.
4. Simmer for a while.
5. Add the optional cream.

It's as easy as that. I often hear the excuse that today's modern housewife (or househusband for that matter) doesn't have time to make his or her own soup. It takes less than half an hour to make enough hearty soup to serve 10 to 12 people. A can will only serve 2 people, 3 if they are not very hungry.

Once you have mastered the principles then you can experiment with all sorts of combinations of vegetables and herbs. Don't be frightened of herbs, they are so easy to use and they add something special that makes a soup singing with flavour!

Try and get into the habit of making more soup than you need and freeze what you don't use on the day of making. If you only have a small freezer, halve the recipe given and freeze before you add the cream to save space.

Homemade soup is warm and appetising and it is a welcoming start to any meal. A thick nourishing broth can be a complete meal in itself.

Try and use butter as opposed to margarine because it will give the soup a far fuller flavour. Hopefully I will have persuaded you, by the end of this book, that the worst butter is far superior to the best margarine!

Don't be afraid to mix and match 'like-minded' soups. I often combine two soups to create a completely new flavour.

Be Adventurous. Go for It!

'NEW FARM' SOUPS & BROTHS

LEEK & POTATO

CARROT, ORANGE & FRESH MINT

SMOKED HADDOCK & FENNEL

CARROT & CARAWAY

POTATO & BAYLEAF

TOMATO & BASIL

BARLEY BROTH WITH CARROTS & CREAM

MUSHROOM, CREAM, TARRAGON & CIDER

CREAM OF CAULIFLOWER & CHEDDAR CHEESE

BULB FENNEL & CUCUMBER

SOUPS & BROTHS

LEEK & POTATO SOUP

Grow your own leeks and you will never be without a soup or easily cooked vegetable in the winter. Better still, grow a few potatoes and you will be well on the way to a whole meal. Leek and potato soup is a classic farmhouse soup and can be dressed up or down for either an everyday soup or a dinner party starter. It also freezes very well.

1½ lbs leeks
2 lbs potatoes
3 ozs butter
3 tablespoons cold water
¾ pint double cream
5 ozs mature cheddar cheese
a little milk
chopped parsley (optional)
   chicken or vegetable stock to cover (1 to 2 pints)

- Trim and chop the leeks into ¼ inch dice. Wash the leeks thoroughly in a colander.
- Wash the potatoes well and chop into ¼ inch dice. (If the quality is good there is no need to peel.)
- In a large pan sweat the leeks in the butter and 3 tablespoons of water for about 5 minutes until the leeks start to soften.
- Add the potatoes to the sweated leeks and cook for a further 5 minutes, stirring occasionally.
- Add enough stock to barely cover the 'leeky potatoes'.
- Cover with a lid and simmer gently for 30 to 40 minutes, stirring occasionally until the potatoes are soft. Check and adjust the seasoning.
- For an everyday soup serve at this stage.
- OR FOR SOMETHING EXTRA SPECIAL...
- Whilst stirring add the double cream thinned with a little milk.
- Grate the cheddar cheese and stir into the soup.
- Check and adjust the seasoning. (More cheese? More stock?)
- Keep warm until ready to serve. Strew with chopped parsley.

A Farmhouse Classic!

CARROT, ORANGE AND FRESH MINT SOUP

1½ lbs carrots
1 large onion
1 large potato
2 ozs butter
3 tablespoons cold water
2 sweet & juicy oranges
1½ to 2½ pints hot chicken or vegetable stock
fresh mint

- Roughly chop the peeled carrots, onion, and the peeled potato.
- In a large saucepan sweat the onion with the butter and the 3 tablespoons of water for 5 minutes with the lid on.
- When the onion is soft, but not coloured, add the carrots, potato and <u>one</u> whole orange. Stir and cook for 2 minutes.
- Add the stock to barely cover the vegetables.
- Gently simmer (with the lid on) for 20 to 40 minutes, until the vegetables are cooked.
- Remove the orange and liquidize the vegetables until smooth.
- Add the juice and pulp of the cooked orange but not the rind.
- Liquidize again.
- Finely scissor-snip a generous handful of fresh mint leaves and add to the soup.
- Check the taste. (More orange? More stock? More mint?)
- Thinly slice the second orange and stud the centre of each slice with a small sprig of fresh mint.
- Serve in a large pot, decorated with the minty orange slices floating down the centre.
- Keep warm until serving but serve piping hot with an optional swirl of double cream or yoghurt and mint mayonnaise dressing (see index).

So Light and so Fresh Tasting!

SOUPS & BROTHS

SMOKED HADDOCK AND FENNEL BROTH

Like most herbs, fennel is so easy to grow. Mind you, it does grow quite tall and takes up a fair amount of space. So, if you are unable to grow it just miss it out from this recipe. Don't be afraid to make this amount. It will easily serve 6 to 10 people with plenty left over to whack into the freezer – much nicer than a tin of soup!

2 large onions	1 pint double cream
2 ozs butter	a little milk
5 tablespoons cold water	4 ozs mature cheddar cheese
2½ lbs potatoes	1 tablespoon fresh herb fennel
5 to 7 smoked haddock fillets	

chicken or vegetable stock to cover well (2 to 3 pints)

- Peel and finely dice the onions. Sweat in the butter and water in a large pan with the lid on for 5 minutes.
- Wash the potatoes well and chop into small, even-sized pieces (roughly ¼ inch dice). If good quality, don't peel.
- Stir the potatoes into the sweated onions and cook for a couple of minutes.
- Add stock to cover and simmer until the potatoes are tender.
- Remove the skin and any bones and cut the smoked haddock into 2-inch chunks. Add to the soup and simmer for 5 minutes. (Don't worry, the haddock will cook!)
- Stir in the double cream thinned with a little milk.
- Grate the cheddar cheese and stir into the soup.
- Check and adjust the taste. (More cheese? More cream?)
- Keep warm until ready to serve. Try not to boil again.
- Just before taking to the table, stir in the scissor-chopped fennel and, for presentation, float a whole 'feather' of fennel on the top of the soup.

A Meal in a Pan!

SOUPS & BROTHS

CARROT & CARAWAY SOUP

1 large onion
2 ozs butter
3 tablespoons cold water
1 lb carrots
1 tablespoon dried caraway seeds
1½ to 2 pints chicken or vegetable stock
½ pint double cream

- Peel and finely dice the onion.
- In a large saucepan sweat the onion with the butter and the 3 tablespoons of water for 5 minutes with the lid on the pan.
- Whilst the onions are sweating, peel and grate the carrots using the coarse grater on the food processor.
- When the onion is soft, but not coloured, add the carrots and the caraway seeds. Stir and cook for 2 minutes.
- Add the stock to barely cover the carrots.
- Gently simmer (with the lid off) for 20 to 40 minutes, until the carrots are cooked and the stock has slightly reduced.
- Add the cream and liquidize until smooth.
- Taste and adjust the seasoning. (Maybe add a little more stock or cream.)
- Serve piping hot with an optional swirl of yoghurt and mint mayonnaise dressing (see index).

This can easily be served as an everyday lunchtime soup or with a little swirl of dressing or cream, and maybe a sprig of herbs floating on the top, be jazzed up for a dinner party. Decoration and presentation can turn an everyday dish into something really extra special. Just choose your prettiest serving dishes and look out to the garden for inspiration.

Colourfully Aromatic!

SOUPS & BROTHS

POTATO & BAYLEAF BROTH

A close friend of mine, Susan McKay, has a wonderful health food shop, 'The Grapevine', on the Isle of Bute. She has been supplying 'New Farm' ever since I moved to the island. One day her suppliers sent her 2 kilos of bayleaves by mistake! This broth is the result! Have a guess how big the bag was? Put it this way, I won't have to trim any bay trees for a while!

2 large onions
1½ lbs potatoes
3 ozs butter
5 tablespoons cold water
10 bayleaves
¾ pint double cream
a little milk
4 ozs mature cheddar cheese
chicken or vegetable stock to cover (2 to 3 pints)

- Peel, dice and finely chop the onions.
- Wash the potatoes well, and cut into ¼ inch dice. (If the quality is good there is no need to peel.)
- Sweat the onions in the butter and 5 tablespoons of water for 5 to 10 minutes until the onions start to soften.
- Add the potatoes to the sweated onions and cook for a further 5 minutes, stirring occasionally.
- Add the bayleaves and enough stock to cover the broth well.
- Cover and simmer gently for 20 to 30 minutes until the potatoes are soft, stirring occasionally.
- Fish out the bayleaves and put to one side. Make sure you get them all!
- Liquidize until smooth then return the bayleaves to the soup.
- Whilst stirring add the double cream thinned with a little milk.
- Grate the cheddar cheese and stir into the soup.
- Check and adjust the seasoning. (More cheese? More stock?)
- Keep warm until ready to serve. Try not to boil again.
- Advise your guests <u>not</u> to eat the bayleaves!

My Editor Loves this One!

TOMATO & BASIL SOUP

*This is the nearest I get to a 'tinned' soup in so much as I use tinned tomatoes (the 15 oz size) as opposed to fresh. Lately, I have taken to serving it with **Margaret Browne's** Savoury Onion Scones (see index). It's a perfect combination. However, as you will see in later recipes, this soup can also be used as a tomato and basil sauce.*

2 large onions
2 cloves garlic
2 ozs butter
5 tablespoons cold water

4 tins tomatoes
1/2 tablespoon dried basil
1/4 pint <u>strong</u> chicken stock
1/2-3/4 pint double cream

- Peel and roughly chop the onions. (The soup is liquidized later so no need to be too fussy.)
- Crush the garlic with the flat of a knife. Chop small.
- In a large saucepan gently sweat the onions and garlic with the butter and the water (the lid on the pan) for 3 to 5 minutes.
- Whilst the onions are sweating, open the tins of tomatoes.
- When the onions are soft, but not coloured, add the basil.
- Add the tomatoes. Half fill the last empty tin of tomatoes with cold water. Wash out all the other tins, pouring from one tin to the next. Put the resulting watery juice into the soup.
- Add the stock and stir.
- Put the lid on and gently simmer for 15 to 20 minutes.
- Carefully pulse liquidize. (I always like to leave this soup 'rustic' i.e. not too smooth but with a little bit of 'bite'.)
- Just before serving add the cream. Heat through again.
- Taste and adjust the seasoning. (More stock? More cream?)
- Serve with some yoghurt and mint mayonnaise dressing drizzled over the soup (see index).

Use as a Soup or as a Sauce!

SOUPS & BROTHS

BARLEY BROTH WITH CARROTS AND CREAM

This is not a soup for frail old ladies. One spoonful and they will not want to eat again for a week! Neither is it really suitable for a dinner party. This is a working man's midday meal. It will certainly line his stomach!

1 large onion	3/4 lb potatoes
2 medium leeks	3 large carrots
2 ozs butter	4 tablespoons pearl barley
3 tablespoons cold water	fresh parsley

strong chicken or vegetable stock to cover (about 2 pints)
1/2 pint double cream
mature cheddar cheese

- Peel, dice and finely and evenly chop the onion.
- Trim and chop the leeks into 1/4 inch dice and wash well.
- Sweat the onion and leeks in the butter and 3 tablespoons of water for 5 to 10 minutes until they start to soften.
- Wash the potatoes and carrots well and chop into 1/4 inch dice. (If the quality is good there is no need to peel.)
- Add the potatoes and carrots to the sweated onion and leeks and cook for another 5 minutes, stirring occasionally.
- Add the barley and enough stock to cover the vegetables well.
- Simmer gently for about an hour, with a lid, stirring occasionally until the potatoes and barley are cooked. Barley absorbs a lot of liquid so you may need to add a little more stock. Taste and adjust the seasoning if necessary
- Serve at this stage for an everyday soup.
- For a richer soup, add the double cream.
- Keep warm and when ready to serve, strew with some grated mature cheddar cheese and lots of fresh chopped parsley.

You can Stand your Spoon up in This!

MUSHROOM, CREAM, TARRAGON AND CIDER SOUP

2 large onions
2 cloves garlic
2 ozs butter
3 tablespoons cold water
14 ozs mushrooms
½ tablespoon dried tarragon
2 ozs cream cheese (Philadelphia, or Boursin)
½ to 1 pint double cream
¼ pint cider
¾ pint chicken or vegetable stock

- Peel and dice the onions into small, even-sized pieces.
- Crush the garlic with the flat of a knife. Chop very small.
- In a large saucepan sweat the onions and garlic together with the butter and the water (with the lid on) for 5 minutes.
- Whilst the onions are sweating, finely chop the mushrooms.
- When the onions are soft, but not coloured, add the tarragon and the cream cheese. Stir and cook for 1 minute.
- Add the chopped mushrooms. Stir and cook for 2 minutes.
- Keep stirring. Add the cream, cider and the stock.
- The mushrooms will rise to the top but don't worry they will soon disperse throughout the soup.
- Gently simmer for 20 to 30 minutes.
- Taste and adjust the seasoning and consistency. (More cream? More cider?)

This soup has a most delicious flavour that is quite unusual. I have deliberately made enough to serve at least 10 people because, even with the high cream content, it freezes really well. (Reheat slowly after freezing.) I use this soup recipe as a sauce in the Mushroom, Cream, Tarragon and Cider Stuffed Crepes (see index).

A Soup with a Difference!

SOUPS & BROTHS

CREAM OF CAULIFLOWER AND CHEDDAR CHEESE SOUP

On the farm springtime is always hectic. Lambing and calving take precedence over the garden, so I always end up planting all my vegetables on one day. This leads to seasonal gluts! When this happens I tend to make lots of soups for the freezer. I make this soup when the caulis all come at once. It works just as well with broccoli. Do try to find a source of a good quality <u>mature</u> cheese. You will only need to use a small amount of a strongly flavoured cheese, so it works out a lot cheaper. (The cheese I use comes from the Isle of Bute Creamery. They mature their cheese for 10 to 14 months before they allow it to be sold!)

2 large onions
2 ozs butter
5 tablespoons cold water
2 or 3 heads of cauliflower
½ to 1 pint double cream
6 ozs mature cheddar cheese
1 tbsp fresh chopped dill (optional)
chicken/veg stock to cover (2-3 pints)

- Chop the onions and sweat in the butter and water in a large pan with a lid on.
- Chop the cauliflower into florets and wash well.
- Stir the florets into the sweated onions and cook for a couple of minutes.
- Add stock to barely cover the vegetables and simmer until the cauliflower is tender.
- Carefully pulse liquidize. (I always like to leave the soup 'rustic' i.e. not too smooth but with a little bit of 'bite'.)
- Stir in the double cream.
- Grate the cheddar cheese and stir into the soup.
- Check and adjust the taste. (More Cheese? More Stock?)
- Keep warm until ready to serve.
- Just before taking to the table to serve, stir in the dill.

Creamy and Cheesy!

SOUPS & BROTHS

BULB FENNEL AND CUCUMBER SOUP

1 large cucumber
2 bulbs of fennel
1 large onion
2 ozs butter
4 tablespoons cold water
1½ to 2 pints cold water
¼ pint double cream
½ tablespoon fresh mint
salt and freshly ground black pepper
fresh strawberries

- Wash and chop the cucumber (do not peel).
- Wash and chop the fennel, reserving a 'feather' for garnish.
- Peel and roughly chop the onion.
- In a large pan, sweat the onion and the fennel in the butter and 4 tablespoons of water, for 5 minutes (with a lid on).
- Add the cucumber and cook for one minute.
- Add enough cold water to barely cover the vegetables and simmer for 30 to 40 minutes.
- Liquidize until smooth.
- Add the cream.
- Finely scissor-chop the mint and stir in well.
- Taste and season with plenty of salt and black pepper.
- Serve hot. Just before bringing to the table (and no sooner) add slices of fresh strawberries, about one strawberry per serving, and decorate with the reserved 'feather' of fennel.
- Any leftovers can be served the next day as a chilled summer soup decorated with thin slices of cucumber and mint sprigs.

A Delicate Dinner Party Delight!

'NEW FARM' SALADS

The 'grazing buffet table' at lunchtime offers plenty of opportunity to 'go mad with salad'. From about 12.15pm through until 3.00pm guests meander in for a bite to eat.

I used to employ someone to help with lunches until two days running no guests turned up and I still had wages to pay. So I decided to let the guests do some of the work i.e. lay their own table, serve their own soup and clear their own dishes. Therefore lunch has now become the model of informality. Often I have to physically stop the guests from loading the dishwasher!

The 'grazing table' consists of soup to start followed by a buffet of 3 or 4 hot and cold main courses, 4 or 5 salads, dips and dressings (hot and cold) a huge platter of local Scottish cheeses and 4 or 5 desserts/puddings or cakes. This is rounded off by a bottomless pot of tea or coffee. The guests can eat as much as they like and can sit for as long as they like. They bring their own wine and sit at a big communal table, and they seem to enjoy it! As they wander in you will hear the odd one turn to their partner and say "I'm not really very hungry", and "Could we possibly have a table on our own?". You can guarantee they're the ones that come back for third helpings and are still at the table 3 hours later chatting away to total strangers and having a whale of a time.

Guests very rarely book for lunch so I often have to prepare salads and such as they arrive. I usually make enough in the morning for the first few guests and then make fresh for the latter half of lunch. I do try and carry at least one salad through to the evening meal, usually coleslaw for crunch or maybe a carrot salad for colour depending on what I'm cooking that evening.

You will notice that in some recipes I cheat and use bought mayonnaise or salad cream. This is because they do give salads an extra lease of life in the fridge, buying me some time to cope with the numbers that turn up, often unexpectedly, at 'New Farm Restaurant'.

You really can have fun with salads - sweet, savoury almost anything goes so long as it has colour, flavour, and usually a crunch.

Go Mad with Salad!

'NEW FARM' SALADS

HOT POTATO & FRESH THYME

CRUNCHY CAULIFLOWER

BARLEY, APRICOT & MINT VINAIGRETTE

BEETROOT VINAIGRETTE MOULD

CRISP APPLE & GINGER

BEETROOT, CARROT & COURGETTE

PINEAPPLE & PUMPKIN SEED COLESLAW

CARROT & CARAWAY SEED

MOTHER'S WET SALAD

CARROT SALAD

TOSSED TOMATO VINAIGRETTE

APPLE, MINT & MELON

SALADS

HOT POTATO & FRESH THYME SALAD

At the height of the season I tend to make this salad most days. Why? Because I'm basically lazy! I make a big pot in the late afternoon and serve it hot for dinner. The remainder makes a lovely salad for tomorrow's 'grazing' buffet table. Don't be restricted to fresh thyme - chives, oregano or marjoram work equally well. When the herbs are in flower use the colourful petals to decorate the salad.

1½ lbs potatoes
a pinch of salt
a generous handful of fresh thyme stalks
1 small onion
salad cream

- Wash the potatoes and cut into 2-inch cubes. (If the quality is good there's no need to peel.)
- Cover with plenty of water and a pinch of salt.
- Boil until tender.
- Whilst the potatoes are cooking, peel and <u>very</u> finely dice the onion and strip the thyme leaves from the stalks.
- When cooked, drain the potatoes.
- Add the thyme leaves and the raw onion to the hot potatoes.
- Pour in plenty of salad cream and fold everything together while still hot, breaking up the potatoes a little.
- Serve decorated with more fresh thyme.
- When cold this salad will keep for up to three days in an airtight container in the fridge.
- It reheats well so can be served as a hot vegetable as opposed to a salad.

Is it a Vegetable or is it a Salad?

CRUNCHY CAULIFLOWER SALAD

This is a great salad for those occasions when you have lots of people coming for a meal. Choose the size of your cauli according to the numbers you wish to serve and adjust the quantities of the rest of the recipe as well.

1 cauliflower
1 eating apple
1 carrot
1 head of celery
1 very small onion
juice of a lemon
6 tablespoons mayonnaise (see index)
6 tablespoons natural yoghurt (see index)
1 teaspoon curry paste
fresh chives

- Wash and divide the cauliflower into very small florets.
- Core and quarter the apple (do not peel).
- *Finely* slice or grate the apple.
- Top, tail, peel and grate the carrot.
- Wash and chop the celery.
- Peel and very finely chop the onion.
- Toss all the prepped vegetables in the lemon juice.
- Make the dressing by combining the mayonnaise, natural yoghurt and the curry paste.
- Pour the dressing over the vegetables and mix well.
- Strew with plenty of snipped fresh chives.
- If your chives are flowering, remove the purple petals from the flower heads and sprinkle over the salad.

A Cracking Good Crunch!

SALADS

BARLEY, APRICOT & MINT VINAIGRETTE

No dried apricots, then use tinned - don't forget to drain them! No apricots at all, then use tinned pineapple pieces. I've never been able to cook rice successfully and barley is much more 'farmhouse'.

8 tablespoons pearl barley
15 dried, no-soak apricots
8 tblsps farmhouse vinaigrette
fresh applemint

- Wash the barley and transfer to a large pan.
- Add enough cold water to cover the barley by 2 inches.
- Bring to the boil and simmer until tender.
- Meanwhile, make the vinaigrette (see index) and set aside.
- Roughly chop the apricots and set aside.
- When the barley is cooked, drain well.
- Whilst the barley is still hot stir in the apricots and the vinaigrette.
- Finely scissor-chop a generous handful of applemint leaves.
- Stir the mint into the barley salad.
- Serve piled high on a platter decorated with sprigs of mint.

BEETROOT VINAIGRETTE MOULD

sachet of gelatine powder
1 lb freshly cooked, peeled beetroot
malt vinegar

- Soften the gelatine with warmed vinegar. (Check the gelatine packet for quantity of water and use vinegar instead of water.)
- Add the chopped beetroot.
- Pour into a mould and refrigerate until set.
- Flash dip in hot water for 2 to 3 seconds and turn out on to a serving platter.

CRISP APPLE & GINGER SALAD

3 Granny Smith apples
2 tablespoons orange juice
2 teaspoons grated fresh ginger
2 teaspoons runny honey
1 tablespoon sesame seeds
1 tablespoon white wine vinegar
1 teaspoon whole grain mustard

- Core and quarter the apples (do not peel).
- Finely slice the apples by hand or using the food processor.
- Combine the orange juice, ginger, vinegar, mustard and honey.
- Immediately pour over the apples to prevent them going brown.
- Add the sesame seeds and toss well.

Crisp, Sweet and Gingery!

BEETROOT, CARROT & COURGETTE SALAD

Raw Beetroot }
Carrots   } in equal quantities
Courgettes   }
Mayonnaise

- Wash, peel and grate the uncooked beetroot and carrots.
- Wash and grate the courgettes but do not peel.
- Combine all the vegetables in a bowl.
- Add plenty of mayonnaise (homemade or bought) and mix well.
- Leave to stand for at least an hour to allow the flavours to develop and the colourful juices to run.
- Transfer to a serving dish and decorate with some greenery from the garden.

In the Pink!
A Colourful Addition to Any Table!

SALADS

PINEAPPLE & PUMPKIN SEED COLESLAW

Both of these salads taste much better if they are made a few hours before serving. This gives the flavours time to infuse. (Let the juices flow!) They will keep up to three days if stored in the fridge in an airtight container.

1 tin pineapple pieces
1 white cabbage
2 tablespoons pumpkin seeds
mayonnaise (For this one I use 'Hellmann's'.)

- Drain the juice from the pineapple pieces.
- Finely slice the cabbage (by hand or machine).
- Add the pineapple pieces and pumpkin seeds to the cabbage.
- Add the mayonnaise.
- Mix well and check that the coleslaw is not too dry (the wetter the better).
- To serve, transfer to a platter or serving dish and strew with more pumpkin seeds.

CARROT & CARAWAY SEED SALAD

carrots
caraway seeds
mayonnaise (homemade or bought)

- Top, tail, peel and grate the carrots.
- Add a light sprinkling of caraway seeds to the carrots.
- Toss in plenty of mayonnaise. (It shouldn't be too dry.)
- If you have time leave to infuse.

The Wetter the Better!

MOTHER'S WET SALAD

This recipe has been in my family for generations. Traditionally it was served every Sunday at suppertime with the leftover roast. Within the family it's now become more special than the roast! I've been known to travel over 350 miles to my Mother's home if I know it's going to be on the table!

1 large tomato
1 egg
2 heads of lettuce
1 <u>very small</u> onion
3 inch piece of cucumber
1 oz caster sugar
¼ pint white wine vinegar
juice of ½ lemon
a pinch of dry mustard
4 tablespoons double cream
salt and pepper

- Skin the tomato by immersing in boiling water. After a few minutes the skin will easily slip off. Cut the tomato in half.
- Hard boil the egg. Remove the shell, cool and cut in half.
- Wash and drain the lettuce. Peel the onion and cut in half.
- Place the skinned tomato, boiled egg, lettuce, onion and the unpeeled cucumber in a food processor.
- Pulse chop until well combined but <u>not smooth</u>. Do not liquidize the texture and 'bite' out of it!
- Transfer to a bowl.
- Add the sugar, vinegar, lemon juice, mustard and cream.
- Stir to combine.
- Season with salt and pepper to taste.

Salad, Dip or Dressing?
The Choice is Yours!

SALADS

CARROT SALAD

As its simple name suggests, this salad is very easy to make! The combination of carrots, orange and mustard works very well. The additional splashes of green from the cress and spring onions make it a colourful salad to dress any buffet table.

4 large crisp carrots
3 spring onions
1 punnet of cress
juice of 1 lemon & 1 orange
1 teaspoon whole grain mustard
3 teaspoons honey
1½ tablespoons olive oil
1 tablespoon chopped fresh parsley
salt and freshly ground black pepper

- Top, tail, peel and coarsely grate the carrots.
- Finely chop the spring onions.
- Add the spring onions and the cress to the carrots.
- Make the dressing by combining all the remaining ingredients.
- Pour the dressing over the carrots and toss well.

TOSSED TOMATO VINAIGRETTE

tomatoes
farmhouse vinaigrette (see index)

- With a serrated knife finely slice the tomatoes.
- Put into a serving dish and drizzle with vinaigrette.
- Strew with freshly chopped herbs and lightly toss.

A Riot of Colour!

APPLE, MINT & MELON SALAD
(GREEN SALAD)

This is a stunning salad that never fails to impress. The fruity juices combine to make a memorable, mouth-watering concoction! This salad excites at least three of our senses – the eyes, the nose and the taste buds!

1 galia melon
1 kiwi fruit
1 avocado pear
1 green eating apple
1 cucumber
1 large bunch seedless green grapes
juice of a lemon
6 sprigs of applemint (leaves stripped from stalks)

- Halve the melon and remove the seeds. Cut into slices and remove the skin.
- Chop the melon slices into ½ inch cubes.
- Peel the kiwi fruit and the avocado and chop into ½ inch cubes.
- Wash, quarter and core the apple. Cut into ½ inch cubes.
- Chop the cucumber into ½ inch cubes. Do not peel.
- If the grapes are large cut in half.
- Put all the above into a large bowl and mix well with the lemon juice and lots of finely chopped applemint.
- Leave the salad to rest in the fridge for at least an hour to allow the flavours to mingle and the juices to flow.
- Spoon into a serving dish. I sometimes serve this in a tall, cut glass vase, which shows the salad off well.
- Decorate the top of the salad with a sprig of mint and a twist of lemon.

A Clean, Fresh Flavour!

'NEW FARM' VEGETABLES

We have quite a large vegetable garden at 'New Farm'. We are not organic but we do care how we fight the never-ending battle with weeds, pests and diseases. We are now trying 'companion' planting. This means growing marigolds alongside cabbages, for example. I think the theory is that the dreaded pest the cabbage white fly is supposed to be attracted to the colourful, highly perfumed marigold and not the growing vegetables. Well that may be the theory, I'm not sure whether it works but it makes the vegetable patch look very pretty.

Not only do we share the vegetable patch with pests, diseases and weeds but also a couple of dozen free-range hens. So you can guarantee ours is not a garden that garden-lovers aspire to, such as those seen on TV. It is usually in a rather sorry state. Just when it is looking at its worst a kind-hearted gardener takes pity on the struggling vegetables. Armed with a trowel and fork, within a couple of hours the garden has what is known these days as a 'make-over'. Garden-lovers seem to get a lot of satisfaction out of weeding and tidying. All I get is a bad back! I always seem to start the spring season off with good intentions and great ideas. The spirit is willing but the aching muscles are not!

That being said I am not a fan of frozen veg, with the exception of frozen whole green beans and of course frozen peas. I did try growing peas once but the birds had a better feast than the guests. Now I only grow a few rows and, once picked I serve them piled high, still raw and in their pods, on a large platter at the buffet lunch table.

Serving peas in this way brings a whole new meaning to *'al-dente'*, the term usually used to describe the stage at which vegetables are cooked to retain their colour and most of their crunch. This is only achieved by rapid cooking, almost at the last minute. In smart restaurants they do this by cooking the veg in the morning, cooling them rapidly in cold water and then microwaving them for a couple of minutes just prior to serving. For a dinner party you could do this at home but I don't recommend it for everyday cooking. I'm not sure what the effect is on the vitamin and mineral content of the vegetables. Much better to plan ahead and do what I do. Cook a couple of veg in the oven and the rest just before serving.

Keep the Colour & Most of the Crunch!

VEGETABLES

'NEW FARM' VEGETABLES

LEEK & POTATO MASH

FARMHOUSE RATATOUILLE

CURLY KALE & GINGER BUTTER

AGA STYLE POTATOES

ROASTED PARSNIPS

'WOODEND' AUBERGINES

BRAISED RED CABBAGE WITH CRAB APPLE JELLY

CARAWAY CABBAGE

GREEN BEANS & GARLIC

FENNEL POTATOES

WILD GARLIC POTATOES

CARROTS & CARAWAY

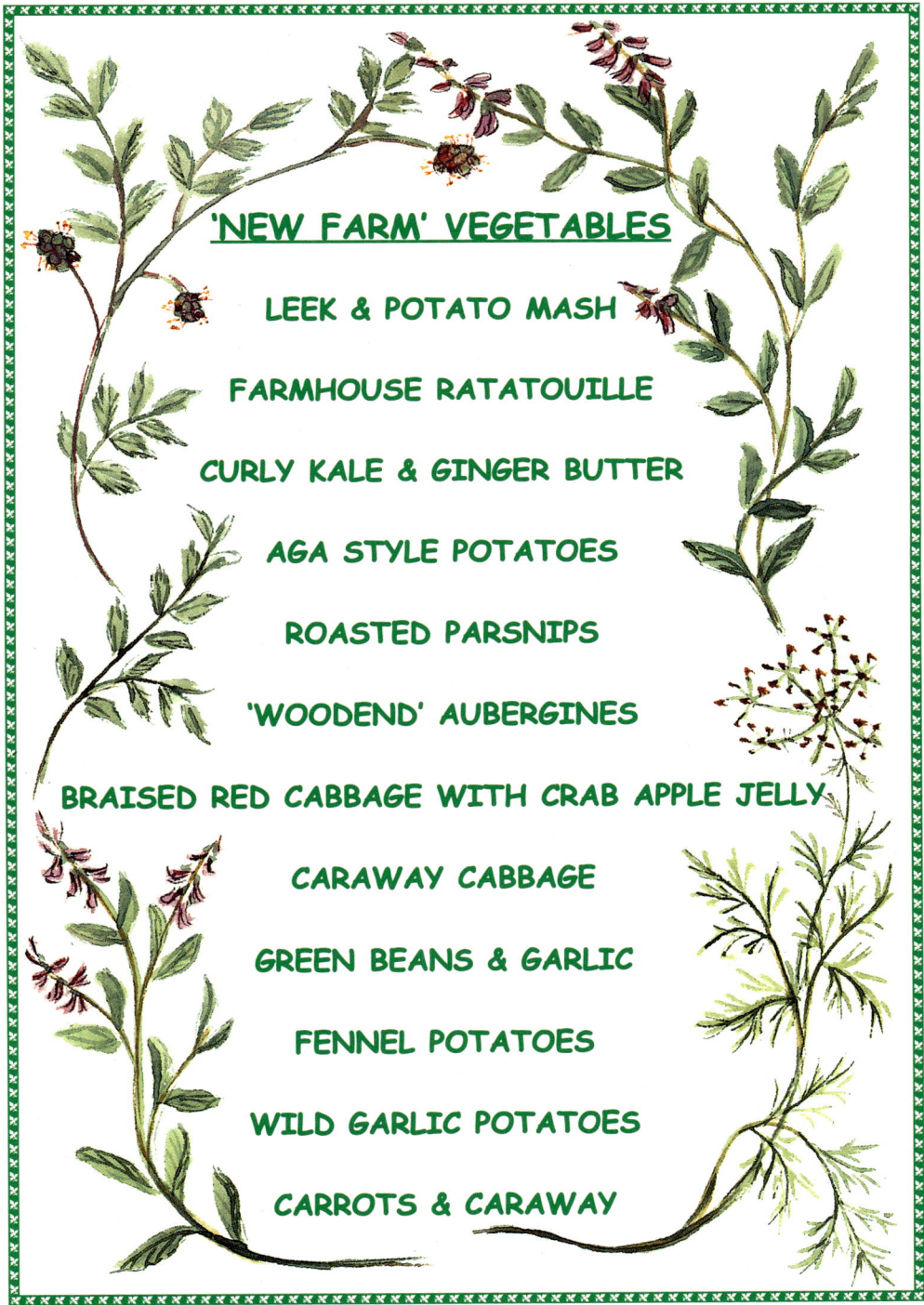

VEGETABLES

LEEK & POTATO MASH

2 lbs potatoes
12 ozs leeks
5 ozs butter
2 tablespoons water
salt and pepper
nutmeg

- Wash and peel the potatoes.
- Chop into even-sized pieces.
- Boil until tender.
- Cut the leeks into 1/4 inch dice and wash well.
- Cook the leeks gently in 2 ozs butter and water with a lid on until tender, stirring every few minutes. Do not drain.
- As soon as the potatoes are cooked, drain them thoroughly and mash well.
- Mix the potatoes and the buttery leeks together.
- Beat a little more butter into the mashed potatoes and leeks to give a soft, smooth but firm texture.
- Season with a little salt, lots of black pepper and a little freshly grated nutmeg.
- Transfer to a hot serving dish.
- Make a well in the centre of the mash and drop in a large knob of butter (about 2 ozs) so it melts and forms a puddle.

In Ireland whole books are devoted to the humble potato. They have the most wonderful names for these potato dishes. The recipe above is usually referred to as leek champ but it could just as easily have been chive champ, nettle champ, parsley champ or pea champ. The Irish have another wonderful potato dish called colcannon. It's very similar to champ but usually uses spring greens. The secret of both champ and colcannon is to serve them immediately in a hot dish with a lump of butter melting to form a puddle in the centre.

FARMHOUSE RATATOUILLE

Traditional ratatouille uses aubergines but as they are a wee bit difficult to grow on a wet Scottish island I've just left them out. Fresh tomatoes taste a lot nicer than tinned but I'm not very good at growing them either!
I sometimes decorate this dish with courgette flowers. Check that there are no wee beasties lurking inside the folded petals!

2 onions
3 medium leeks
3 courgettes
1 clove garlic

2 ozs butter
5 tablespoons cold water
3 tins chopped tomatoes
2 tsps dried mixed herbs (optional)

a little salt and sugar to season

- Peel, halve and slice the onions lengthways.
- Thinly slice the leeks into rings and wash well.
- Wash and slice the courgettes into ¼ inch rings.
- Peel and finely chop the garlic.
- Sweat the onions and garlic in butter and water for 3 minutes with a lid on the pan.
- Add the leeks. Cover and sweat for another 3-4 minutes, stirring occasionally.
- Add the courgettes and cook for one more minute.
- Add enough tinned tomatoes to cover the vegetables.
- Add your dried herbs if desired. (Depending on how I feel, I use either mixed dried herbs, dried basil or dried oregano!)
- Bring to the boil and simmer, covered for 20 minutes.
- Cook until the liquid is reduced and thickened. To be honest, the longer this cooks the better!
- Season with salt and a little sugar to taste.
- Serve hot or cold. This dish also reheats very well and usually tastes even better the second time around.

A Technicolour Treat!

VEGETABLES

CURLY KALE & GINGER BUTTER

I have never been a fan of curly kale until recently when it was served at a Burns supper that I attended. The host had dressed the kale in ginger butter and it was delicious. So much so that when, like 'Oliver', I asked for some more I was too late. Someone else had got there before me.

Burns suppers are held towards the end of January as close to the 25th as possible. This is the date of Robert Burns birthday. He is the national bard (poet) of Scotland and although he died over 200 years ago his birth is still celebrated all over the world. Traditionally the celebration consists of a supper of haggis, neeps (turnips) and tatties (potatoes) but most hosts serve a few other dishes too. The meal is followed by an evening of poetry and recitations.

Curly kale is very easy to cook and goes well with any meaty main course. When cooked it behaves very like spinach and shrinks away to about half its original volume - so make sure you use more than you think you'll actually need!

curly kale
cold water
3 ozs butter
1 inch of root ginger

- Wash the kale and remove the hard rib down the centre of each leaf. This is time consuming but necessary.
- Drain the kale then put it into a large saucepan with about an inch of cold water.
- Cook rapidly, with the lid on, for about 10 minutes.
- When cooked the kale will have shrunk and wilted, but it should still be slightly crunchy.
- Peel and <u>very</u> <u>finely</u> chop the root ginger.
- Mash the ginger into the softened butter
- Toss the cooked curly kale in the ginger butter.
- Serve immediately.

Ginger and Spice and all Things Nice!

AGA STYLE POTATOES

I do most of my cooking on 'Bessy', a very temperamental 56-year-old AGA. An AGA works on a stored heat principal (as opposed to the instant heat of an electric or gas cooker). Therefore, I try and do as much as I can in the oven because when cooking on the top, with the lids open, you lose heat. So most of the dishes that I serve start off on the top of the AGA and finish up in the oven which is exactly how I make AGA style potatoes.

Potatoes OVEN TEMP: 190°C or 375°F or GAS 5
Full cream milk
Garlic (1 clove for each lb of potatoes)
Double cream
Freshly grated nutmeg
Mature cheddar cheese (optional)

- Do not peel the potatoes if the quality is good
- Wash and thinly slice the potatoes.
- Transfer to a large saucepan and cover with milk.
- Add the peeled and finely chopped garlic.
- Simmer <u>very</u> gently for 20 to 30 minutes until soft.
- Drain off the milk (use for another recipe).
- Transfer the cooked, sliced potatoes to a gratin dish.
- Pour enough double cream over the potatoes to leave the top layer cream-free. Grate plenty of nutmeg over the top.
- Pop into the oven and bake for about an hour.
- Ten minutes before the potatoes are ready sprinkle with grated cheese and bake until the cheese is melted and golden.

AGA style potatoes will keep warm for hours without coming to any harm at all. A few potatoes will go a long way when cooked like this. If you want to be really extravagant and push the boat out, you could add some sliced onions at the 'cover with milk' stage.

VEGETABLES

ROASTED PARSNIPS

I always think of parsnips as a slightly overlooked vegetable but they really are quite delicious. During the roasting the starch in the parsnip is changed into sugar giving it a sweet and nutty flavour. Parsnips are very easy to grow and, along with leeks and carrots, they overwinter well in the garden. If you have any fibrous older ones, which have been left too long in the ground, don't roast them. Cut out the hard, inner core and use them to make a purée with a few cooked potatoes, butter, cream, black pepper and lots of nutmeg.

OVEN TEMP: 220°C or 425°F or GAS 7

Parsnips
Cooking oil

- Top, tail and peel the parsnips.
- Cut in half lengthways then continue to cut into even-sized lengths to the thickness of a fat finger!
- Boil till almost tender.
- Drain and cool.
- Pour about ¼ inch of oil into a roasting tin.
- Roll the parsnips in the oil until well coated.
- Ensure that the parsnips are evenly spaced in the tin.
- Roast in a very hot oven for 45 minutes to an hour, turning occasionally.
- With a slotted spoon lift the parsnips into a pre-heated serving dish.
- <u>Serve immediately</u>.
- I usually do my roast potatoes in exactly the same way.

Simple, Sweet and Good!

VEGETABLES

'WOODEND' AUBERGINES

This recipe comes from my dearest friend and Editor, Joan Walters. She lives in a magnificent rambling Georgian mansion, called 'Woodend House', situated by the shores of Loch Fad on our beautiful island, the Isle of Bute.
(By the way she also does excellent Bed & Breakfast at 'Woodend House'.
Tel: 01700 505 619 web site: http://www.isle-of-bute.com)

PREHEAT OVEN: 200°C or 400°F or GAS 6

Aubergines
Garlic (1 clove per aubergine)
Freshly ground sea salt and black pepper
Olive oil

- Wash the aubergines and dice evenly.
- Peel and finely chop the garlic.
- Place the aubergines in an ovenproof dish.
- Scatter over the garlic and plenty of sea salt and pepper.
- Sprinkle generously with olive oil and mix well.
- Roast in a hot oven until the aubergines are tender and the edges are crisp and brown.
- Serve with lots of homemade bread to mop up any juices!

This recipe can be adapted for almost any vegetable – including potatoes which only need to be washed (not peeled) and cut into small, even-sized chunks. It is particularly delicious as a medley of the week's unused veggies. For example, roast a mixture of onions, garlic, peppers, aubergines, mushrooms, courgettes and fresh tomatoes. Again, make sure you serve with plenty of good bread to clean up all the tasty juices! Incidentally, this can be served as a light meal in itself if accompanied with a green salad.

Veggies for Dinner?

VEGETABLES

BRAISED RED CABBAGE WITH CRAB APPLE JELLY

This is a very hearty vegetable dish and has rather fruity undertones. It goes well with meat or poultry. Redcurrant jelly is a good substitute for crab apple jelly.

PREHEAT OVEN: 190°C or 375°F or GAS 5

1 lb red cabbage
1 oz butter
1 onion
1 oz demerara sugar
2 tablespoons crab apple jelly
2 tablespoons cider vinegar or white wine vinegar
1 tablespoon water
1 teaspoon salt
black pepper
1 bayleaf (optional)

- Finely shred the red cabbage.
- Rinse in cold water and drain well.
- Finely chop the onion and cook in the butter for 5 minutes until golden brown.
- Add the demerara sugar and stir until it begins to caramelise. Watch carefully as this happens quite quickly.
- Add the cabbage, crab apple jelly, vinegar, water, salt, black pepper and the bayleaf.
- Bubble for 3 minutes, stirring well to blend.
- Transfer to an ovenproof casserole with a lid.
- Cook for 30 to 40 minutes, stirring half way through.
- Taste and add more salt if necessary. The cabbage should be both sour and sweet and it should also still have a little 'bite'.

Savour the Sweet and Sour!

CARAWAY CABBAGE

Here are two very simple vegetable dishes. They are both cooked in much the same way. I find that preparing vegetables in this way helps to keep their full flavour.

White cabbage
Butter
Caraway seeds

- Peel the outer layers from your cabbage and discard.
- Slice the cabbage thinly.
- Put a large knob of butter into a saucepan. Add the cabbage.
- Lightly sprinkle with caraway seeds.
- Put the lid on your pan and sweat on a high heat.
- Toss the cabbage from time to time until cooked (about 5 minutes - lid on, and a further 2 minutes - lid off). Do not over cook! The cabbage should still be slightly crisp.
- Serve immediately if possible. However, this dish will keep in a warm oven for a short while.

GREEN BEANS AND GARLIC

Frozen green beans   Garlic
Butter   Sesame seeds (optional)

- Peel and finely chop the garlic.
- Put a large knob of butter in a saucepan.
- Add the green beans, garlic and a sprinkling of sesame seeds.
- Sweat with a lid on, for about 5 minutes, plus 2 minutes without the lid, stirring occasionally, until cooked but still semi-crisp.
- To retain the bright green colour, serve immediately.

Sweat up your Veg!

VEGETABLES

FENNEL POTATOES

OVEN TEMP: 190°C or 375°F or GAS 5

2 very large potatoes
1 bulb fennel
1 onion
½ pint chicken stock

- Peel and thinly slice the potatoes.
- Wash and thinly slice the fennel.
- Peel and thinly slice the onion.
- In an ovenproof dish place alternate layers of potato, fennel and onion, starting and ending with potato, seasoning each layer with salt and pepper as you go.
- Barely cover with the chicken stock.
- Cover and cook for 40 to 45 minutes until tender.

WILD GARLIC POTATOES

Throughout the months of May and June you will smell the pungent aroma of the white-flowered wild garlic when out walking in the woods.

Potatoes   Butter
Salt   Milk (optional)
    Wild garlic leaves and flowers

- Peel the potatoes and boil until tender.
- Drain the cooked potatoes and mash with a large knob of butter and a little milk if they seem stiff.
- Scissor-snip the wild garlic leaves and stir into the mashed potatoes. Experiment to see how much wild garlic you like.
- Serve hot decorated with lots of wild garlic flowers.

Anything Goes with Potatoes!

CARROTS & CARAWAY

You will probably have noticed that I am quite partial to caraway seeds, judging by the number of recipes in this book that use them. I find caraway has a lovely aromatic flavour and can be used for either sweet or savoury dishes. I have never tried to grow caraway but I have read that it is quite easy.

Carrots
Caraway seeds
Butter

- Do not peel the carrots if the quality is good.
- Wash and chop the carrots into 2-inch pieces.
- Using the multi-purpose blade of the food processor, chop the carrots down to an eighth of an inch.
- Transfer to a large, microwave-proof bowl.
- Add a sprinkling of caraway seeds and a large knob of butter.
- Microwave on full power for a total of 8-10 minutes in two bursts, stirring halfway through.
- Test until tender but watch out – it's hot!
- Cook this well in advance of your meal because this dish is far superior when re-heated.

Here is another recipe using the above ingredients.

- Choose even sized small carrots (or cut to size).
- Top and tail and peel if you really must.
- Lay each carrot on a piece of foil and sprinkle with about 8 caraway seeds per carrot. Top with a small knob of butter.
- Wrap up each carrot in 'Christmas cracker' fashion.
- Bake in a hot oven for about an hour until cooked and tender.

Delicately Spice up your Carrots!

'NEW FARM' MEATY MAIN COURSES

I've nothing much to say about
'New Farm' Meaty Main Courses
other than, if you are not having a relationship
with a farmer then you really should
be having a relationship with your local butcher...!!!!

Be Best Friends with your Butcher!
(Trust in his judgement and ensure the meat he is
selling is fresh and from local farms.)

'NEW FARM' MEATY MAIN COURSES

LAMB CASSEROLED WITH PLUM TOMATOES, BASIL & BARLEY WITH A BASIL SUET CRUST

PORK CASSEROLED WITH APRICOTS AND TARRAGON SERVED WITH TARRAGON DUMPLINGS

CHERRIED DUCK WITH ORANGE

SAUSAGE AND APPLE PARCELS

BEEF BRAISED IN BROWN ALE WITH BASIL BATTER PUDDINGS

SWEET & SOUR BELLY PORK RIBS

LEMON & THYME STUFFED SHOULDER OF LAMB

SAUSAGEMENT, SAGE & SWEET APPLE PIE

PEPPERED PORK & POTATO PIE

HAM & PINEAPPLE PUDDING

MEATY MAIN COURSES

LAMB CASSEROLED WITH PLUM TOMATOES BASIL & BARLEY WITH A BASIL SUET CRUST

This really is 'rustic farmhouse food'. I recently served this dish to 6 Dutch business men, who were more used to eating in fancy Amsterdam restaurants. When I went back into the dining room to see if everything was OK they gave me a standing ovation. I think that says it all. Try it for yourself and see what reception you get!

2 large onions
3 tablespoons cold water
3 tablespoons pearl barley
1/2 tablespoon dried basil
1 tin chopped plum tomatoes
hot chicken stock to cover
6 ozs self-raising flour
3 ozs suet (Atora)
1/2 teaspoon dried basil
cold water
1 1/2 lbs cubed shoulder or leg of lamb

- Finely slice the onions and sweat in a large pan with the water.
- Add the barley, basil, tomatoes and lamb.
- Add enough <u>boiling hot</u> stock to barely cover the lamb.
- Bring to the boil and cook for 5 minutes.
- Transfer to a large, lidded casserole. Pop it into the oven.
- Cook for 1 1/2 to 2 hours until the barley is cooked and the meat is tender. OVEN TEMP: 190°C or 375°F or GAS 5
- Mix the flour, suet and basil together with enough cold water to form a pastry dough.
- Forty minutes before you wish to serve, remove the lamb from the oven. Roll out the pastry to 1/4 inch thick and fit over the casserole as a lid. Crimp the edges for presentation.
- Pop it back in the oven for half an hour until evenly brown.
- Serve with AGA style potatoes, caraway carrots, green beans with garlic and pineapple pumpkin seed coleslaw (see index).

Old Fashioned Farmhouse Fayre!

PORK CASSEROLED WITH APRICOTS AND TARRAGON SERVED WITH TARRAGON DUMPLINGS

This is a variation on the theme of the previous recipe. Instead of a crust you get dumplings, instead of lamb you get pork and instead of basil you get tarragon! And just to confuse you I've added some apricots! I've always said cooking should be fun!

PREHEAT OVEN: 190°C or 375°F or GAS 5

2 large onions
3 ozs butter
3 tablespoons pearl barley
½ tablespoon dried tarragon
8 dried no-soak apricots
hot chicken stock to cover
6 ozs self-raising flour
3 ozs suet (Atora)
½ teaspoon dried tarragon
cold water
1½ lbs cubed shoulder or leg of pork

- Finely slice the onions. Sweat in a large pan with the butter.
- Add the barley, tarragon, apricots and pork.
- Add enough <u>boiling hot</u> stock to barely cover the pork.
- Bring to the boil and cook for 5 minutes.
- Transfer to a large casserole. Put the lid on the casserole and pop it into the oven.
- Cook for 1½ to 2 hours until the barley is cooked and the meat is tender.
- Mix the flour, suet and tarragon together with enough cold water to form a wet, sticky dough (too wet to handle).
- Thirty minutes before you wish to serve, remove the casserole from the oven. With a dessertspoon, spoon the dumplings evenly on to the top of the pork.
- Pop it back in the oven for half an hour until the dumplings are crisp and evenly brown but please make sure they are thoroughly cooked underneath.

MEATY MAIN COURSES

CHERRIED DUCK WITH ORANGE

If you are unable to lay your hands on a free-range duck, then get hold of a free-range chicken! This recipe also works well with pheasant.

OVEN TEMP: 190°C or 375°F or GAS 5

1 tin stoned cherries
2 oranges
¼ pint chicken stock
1 free-range duck
1 peeled onion
salt

- Put the cherries in a bowl and add the grated rind and juice of 1 orange and the chicken stock. Put to one side.
- Thoroughly wash the duck inside and out.
- Put the onion and the other orange (both cut into quarters) into the cavity of the duck.
- Prick the skin all over with a fork to allow the fat to run out.
- Rub the skin with salt.
- Stand on a rack in a roasting tin and roast for 1½ hours. Drain and discard the fat from the tin.
- Put the duck back into the roasting tin without the rack and pour over the cherry and orange sauce.
- Cover with tin foil and cook for another 1½ hours increasing the heat to 200°C or 400°F or Gas 6.
- Before serving please check that the duck is cooked through.
- Transfer the duck to a warmed serving platter and pour the cherry juices from the roasting tin over the duck to serve.
- Why not decorate with a few orange slices and some greenery?

Cherried Duck! Cherried Chicken!

MEATY MAIN COURSES

SAUSAGE AND APPLE PARCELS

I very rarely do the 'bacon and egg thing' for guests at breakfast time because there is far too much going on first thing in the morning. Another reason is that by the time the guests arrive, they may have been on holiday for a few days already and can't possibly face yet another cooked breakfast. So I tend to serve what I call a 'farmhouse continental'. Guests can arrive any time they wish. Most choose to have a long lie in and come down to more of a brunch than a breakfast. This is one of the dishes I sometimes serve.

PREHEAT OVEN: 190°C or 375°F or GAS 5
GREASED BAKING TRAY

10 ozs plain flour	1 lb pork sausagemeat
1½ teaspoons baking powder	1 cooking apple
5 ozs suet (Atora)	2 tablespoons fruit chutney
salt and pepper	1 beaten egg
cold water to mix	

- Evenly mix the flour, baking powder, suet and seasoning.
- Add enough water to make a soft pliable dough.
- Divide into 8 equal portions and roll out into 6-inch circles.
- Paint the outer edge of each circle with a little water
- Divide the sausagemeat into 8 equal-sized flat rounds.
- Place a round of meat in the centre of each pastry disc.
- Peel and core the apple. Chop into 8 chunks.
- Place an apple chunk and a little chutney on top of the meat.
- Gather up the pastry round the filling to make tight parcels.
- Turn the parcels over and transfer to the baking tray.
- Brush the tops of the parcels with the beaten egg.
- Bake for 30 to 40 minutes, until the pastry is cooked and evenly brown. Serve hot or cold.

Breakfast, Brunch or Supper!

MEATY MAIN COURSES

BEEF BRAISED IN BROWN ALE WITH BASIL BATTER PUDDINGS

This is a superb party dish that can be made from either braising or stewing beef. It is actually better made a day or two in advance, leaving you with just the basil batter puds to make an hour before serving.

OVEN TEMP: 190°C or 375°F or GAS 5

2 large onions
2 ozs butter
3 tablespoons cold water
3 tablespoons pearl barley
1½ lbs cubed beef
1 bottle of Newcastle Brown Ale
a little chicken stock to cover

4 ozs plain flour
½ teaspoon salt
2 eggs
½ pint cold water
4 teaspoons oil
½ teaspoon dried basil
lard

- Peel and finely slice the onions and sweat in a large pan (lid on) with the butter and water.
- Add the barley, beef, Newcastle Brown Ale and enough <u>boiling hot</u> stock to barely cover the beef.
- Bring to the boil and cook for 5 minutes.
- Transfer to a large, lidded casserole. Pop it into the oven.
- Cook for 1½ to 2 hours until the barley is cooked and the meat is tender.
- Put the flour, salt, egg, water, oil and basil into a bowl and beat to make a smooth batter. Refrigerate for an hour.
- Three quarters of an hour before you wish to serve, put a little lard into the 12 individual holes of a bun (muffin) tin.
- Set the oven to 220°C or 425°F or Gas 7. Put the tin in the oven and, when the fat smokes, ¾-fill each hole with the batter. Return to the oven and bake for 20 to 30 minutes.
- Try not to look in the oven until the puds are nearly cooked.
- Place the batter puds on top of the beef and <u>serve at once!</u>

MEATY MAIN COURSES

SWEET & SOUR BELLY PORK RIBS

PREHEAT OVEN: 200°C or 400°F or GAS 6

2 tablespoons demerara sugar
2 tablespoons malt vinegar
1 tablespoon soy sauce
1 tablespoon Worcester sauce
2 tablespoons tomato purée
1 tin pineapple pieces
1/4 teaspoon ground ginger
1/4 pint water
2 onions peeled and chopped
2 tablespoons vegetable oil
2 sheets belly pork ribs (chopped into single ribs)
1 1/2 tablespoons cornflour
3 tablespoons cold water
finely grated rind of 1 orange

- To make the sweet and sour sauce, mix together the sugar, vinegar, soy sauce, Worcester sauce, tomato purée, tin of pineapple (fruit and juice), ginger and water.
- In your <u>largest</u> frying pan, fry the peeled and finely diced onions in the oil. When cooked remove the onions from the pan and place in a large casserole.
- Now fry the pork ribs (a few at a time) and brown evenly.
- Transfer the pork ribs as they are browned to the casserole and pour over the sweet and sour sauce. Put the lid on.
- Put the ribs into the oven and cook till tender (1 1/2 to 2 hours).
- When cooked, remove the ribs. Place on a warmed serving dish and keep hot.
- Dissolve the cornflour in 3 tablespoons of cold water. Then add 5 tablespoons of the hot sweet and sour sauce and stir well.
- Add this mixture to the rest of the sauce. Bring to the boil, stirring, and simmer until thickened.
- Taste and adjust the seasoning.
- Pour a little sauce over the ribs and garnish with grated orange rind and greenery. Serve the rest of the sauce separately.

Messy to Eat but Oh So Good!

MEATY MAIN COURSES

LEMON & THYME STUFFED SHOULDER OF LAMB

Shoulder of lamb is usually a cheaper cut of meat than leg and it is much sweeter and tastier. Ask your butcher to kindly remove the shoulder bone to create a pocket for you to stuff.

OVEN TEMP: 190°C or 375°F or GAS 5

1 large onion	8 ozs fresh breadcrumbs
2 ozs butter	1 egg
3 tablespoons cold water	juice of 1 lemon
12 dried no-soak apricots	1 pint cold water
1 teaspoon dried thyme	apricot jam
grated rind of 1 lemon	demerara sugar

1 boned shoulder of lamb

- Peel and finely slice the onion and sweat in a large pan with the butter and water. Remove from the heat.
- Scissor snip the apricots into small pieces.
- In a large bowl stir the onion, apricots, dried thyme, lemon rind and breadcrumbs together.
- Bind the stuffing mixture with the beaten egg and lemon juice.
- Pack the stuffing into the lamb pocket. Wrap tightly in buttered tin foil.
- Place in a roasting tin with a pint of cold water.
- Roast for 2 to 2½ hours until the meat is tender.
- Carefully remove the foil and brush the shoulder of lamb with apricot jam and sprinkle with demerara sugar.
- Return to the oven for 30 minutes until evenly coloured.
- Make a gravy with the meat juices and serve on a hot platter garlanded with garden greenery.

Stuff it and Roast it!

MEATY MAIN COURSES

SAUSAGEMEAT SAGE & SWEET APPLE PIE

'Meat and sweet' always go so well together and this is no exception. There are <u>never</u> any leftovers and I have yet to see a man take only one portion. Try hard to use fresh sage as opposed to dried - it is far nicer. If you do have to use dried this time, prompt yourself, go on, <u>now</u> is the best time to start some off in the garden.

PREHEAT OVEN: 190°C or 375°F or GAS 5

1 large cooking/eating apples
1 tablespoon cold water
1/2 tablespoon granulated sugar
1/2 mug fresh sage leaves
(or 1 teaspoon dried sage)

1 1/2 lbs pork sausagemeat
2 beaten eggs
lard for greasing
1 recipe quantity of shortcrust pastry (see index)

1 beaten egg + a little milk

- Peel, core and chop the apple and gently cook in the water and sugar until soft. (I often do this in the microwave.)
- Finely scissor-chop the fresh sage leaves.
- In a large bowl mix the sausagemeat, eggs, apple and sage.
- Roll out some of the pastry and line the pie plate.
- Fill the pie with the wettish sausagemeat mixture.
- Roll out the remaining pastry and put a lid on the pie.
- Crimp the edges of the pastry for presentation and to keep the meat within the pie. With scissors, snip a couple of steam holes in the pastry lid. <u>Lightly</u> and evenly brush with a mixture of beaten egg and milk to glaze the pie.
- Bake for 30 to 40 minutes until cooked and evenly brown.
- Remove from the oven. Brush <u>immediately</u> all over with a little more egg glaze. This will give the pie a lovely sheen.
- Serve hot or cold decorated with half an apple pierced with a sprig of sage. This bit is optional but it does look nice!

MEATY MAIN COURSES

PEPPERED PORK & POTATO PIE

I tend to use Gruyere cheese in this recipe because of its melting qualities, but a mature cheddar cheese would work equally well.
The juices from the pork flavour the potatoes. If you have any cooked potatoes left over, make a treat for the next day. Sprinkle with some more cheese and reheat.

OVEN TEMP: 190°C or 375°F or GAS 5
BUTTERED GRATIN DISH

2 large onions
1 oz butter
1 tablespoon olive oil
1 tablespoon cold water
2 lbs potatoes
6 ozs Gruyere or mature cheddar cheese
1 to 1½ pints chicken stock
1 pork chop per guest
salt, black pepper and dried sage

- Peel the onions, cut in half and thinly slice lengthways.
- In a pan sweat the onions in the butter, olive oil and water.
- Wash, peel and thinly slice the potatoes.
- In a gratin dish arrange alternate layers of potato slices, onion and grated cheese (beginning and ending with the potato).
- Barely cover with the stock. Cook in the oven for 30 minutes.
- For each guest take a pork chop and coat it with a mixture of salt and black pepper. Sprinkle with a little dried sage.
- Cover the cooked potatoes with the pork chops and cook for a further 45 minutes to an hour, turning half way through.
- Check that the chops are thoroughly cooked before serving.

Pepper up your Pork!

HAM & PINEAPPLE PUDDING

Don't be confused by the name, this is a savoury dish. It was created when I unsuccessfully tried to make a soufflé! If cooked ham pieces are hard to come by, use cooked chunks of bacon. Drained tinned apricots work just as well as pineapple. It's equally delicious hot or cold. I have put a vegetarian alternative in the 'Veggie, Vegan and Fish' chapter. With a bit of homemade bread and butter and a salad, you've got a really easy meal.

PREHEAT OVEN: 190°C or 375°F or GAS 5

2 large onions	salt and pepper
5 ozs butter	nutmeg
1 tablespoon cold water	5 ozs cooked ham pieces
6 eggs	1/2 tin pineapple pieces
1 pint double cream	6 ozs mature cheddar cheese

- Peel the onions and cut into long, thin slices. Sweat in a large pan with the butter and cold water (the lid on) for 5 minutes.
- When cooked set aside to cool.
- In a large bowl whisk together the eggs and the cream.
- Season with the salt, pepper and generous gratings of nutmeg.
- Add the cooked onions and ham.
- Drain and discard the juice from the pineapple.
- Grate the cheese and add it, together with the pineapple pieces to the 'eggie' mixture.
- Pour into a buttered gratin dish and bake in the oven for 40 to 50 minutes <u>until set and evenly golden</u>.
- Serve with Tomato and Basil Sauce. For this, use the Tomato and Basil Soup recipe but only take it as far as the 'rustic' stage i.e. don't add the cream (see index).

This is Really a Failed Soufflé!

'NEW FARM'
VEGGIE, VEGAN & FISH

Although we are very much a meat-producing farm this chapter has been written for meat-eaters who wouldn't mind a change for the day. I really do enjoy cooking and eating vegetarian food. In fact I was a non-meat eater (as opposed to a vegetarian) for about seven years.

It never ceases to amaze me the number of guests that turn up at my door purporting to be vegetarians who tell me in the next breath "but I do eat chicken and fish"! They are what I would call non-meat eaters. I love fish but I have never really enjoyed chicken. I find that intensively reared birds are only a carrier of flavours, not unlike tofu and soya. As yet we don't rear chickens for the table but I'm sure one day we will.

I find that vegans are the hardest to cook for because of my dependency on quality dairy products and free-range eggs. Guests that are on a gluten-free diet, and there are plenty of them, also make me put my thinking cap on.

I suppose the most difficult guest I ever had, from a dietary point of view, was a man who was a fish-eating almost gluten-free vegetarian. He was wheat, barley and rye intolerant and didn't eat sugar, potatoes or mushrooms. To cap it all he couldn't eat fruit after a meal, it had to be before! Gosh, he could hardly eat anything! I read my entire collection of recipe books and I rang everyone I could think of for advice and menu ideas. I finally came up with Carrot, Orange & Fresh Mint Soup (made without butter), a very simple Loch Fad Trout Risotto followed by a Coconut & Amaretto desserty thing! He seemed to enjoy the meal!

The above paragraph aside, I do find that I have a little bit more fun cooking vegetarian food as opposed to the more conventional 'meat and two veg' because I can be even more adventurous, creative and experimental than usual.

Why not be a Veggie for a Day!

'NEW FARM' VEGGIE, VEGAN & FISH

APRICOT & SCALLION LOAF

STILTON & BROCCOLI BAKE

MUSHROOM & OREGANO CRUMBLE

SMOKED SALMON, SPINACH & GRAPE ROULADE

PINE NUT PARCEL SERVED ON A BED OF FARMHOUSE RATATOUILLE

MUSHROOM, CREAM, TARRAGON & CIDER STUFFED CREPES

MEDLEY OF FISH PIE

FENNEL TROUT SERVED WITH A LEMON CREAM SAUCE

VEGGIE, VEGAN & FISH

APRICOT & SCALLION LOAF

Why scallion? Well, Apricot & Onion Loaf doesn't have quite the same ring to it! Scallions are a variety of the onion family. But I usually just use an ordinary, everyday onion!

PREHEAT OVEN: 190°C or 375°F or GAS 5
GREASED TERRINE DISH

1 onion
12 dried, no-soak apricots
1 beaten egg
8 ozs breadcrumbs
1 heaped teaspoon dried basil
1 dessertspoon oil
1 tablespoon fruit juice (I use either apple or pineapple.)
½ oz butter

- Peel and very finely chop the onion.
- Scissor-snip the apricots into small pieces.
- Thoroughly mix together the onion, apricots, breadcrumbs and dried basil.
- Bind with the egg, oil and fruit juice. At this stage you may have to add a few more breadcrumbs if the mixture is too wet.
- Put into the terrine dish and lightly firm down.
- Dot with butter and cover with foil. Bake for about an hour.
- Serve hot or cold with Tomato & Basil Sauce. (See index under Tomato & Basil Soup but don't add the cream!)

In the meat-eating world this is basically a stuffing which can be served as an accompaniment to lamb or pork. However, it makes a wonderful vegetarian meal when served with Tomato & Basil Sauce.

Convert a Carnivore!

STILTON & BROCCOLI BAKE

This is a vegetarian alternative to the Ham & Pineapple Pudding recipe in the 'Meaty Main Courses' chapter. Once again, it is easy to make and can be eaten hot, warm or cold. It is very versatile because you can substitute almost any vegetable for the broccoli. Why not try grated courgettes? No Stilton, then use cheddar cheese!

PREHEAT OVEN: 190°C or 375°F or GAS 5
BUTTERED GRATIN DISH

2 onions	6 eggs
5 ozs butter	1 pint double cream
1 tablespoon cold water	salt and pepper
12 ozs broccoli	fresh nutmeg

6 ozs Stilton Cheese

- Peel the onions and cut into long, thin slices.
- Sweat in the butter and cold water with a lid on the pan.
- When cooked set aside to cool.
- Remove and discard about 2 inches from the bottom of the broccoli stalk. Divide the rest into small florets.
- Cook the broccoli in a little salted water until just tender.
- Drain and plunge into cold water to retain the colour.
- In a large bowl whisk together the eggs and the cream.
- Season with salt, pepper and generous gratings of nutmeg.
- Add the cooked onions and broccoli.
- Grate the cheese and add it to the 'eggie' mixture.
- Pour into the prepared gratin dish and bake in the oven for 40 to 50 minutes until set and evenly golden.
- Serve with Tomato & Basil Sauce. (See index under Tomato & Basil Soup but don't add the cream.)

A Versatile Veggie Treat!

VEGGIE, VEGAN & FISH

MUSHROOM & OREGANO CRUMBLE

There are no dairy products in Mushroom and Oregano Crumble, so it is ideal for vegans. Neither is there anything 'exotic' in it. All of the ingredients can be bought in your local supermarket.

PREHEAT OVEN: 190°C or 375°F or GAS 5

8 ozs breadcrumbs
4 ozs chopped mixed nuts
4 tablespoons vegetable oil
1 large or 2 small onions
8 ozs mushrooms
3 tins tomatoes
2 teaspoons dried oregano

- Mix together the breadcrumbs and the chopped nuts.
- Fry in 3 tablespoons of the oil until evenly golden.
- You may need a little extra oil depending on how absorbent the breadcrumbs are. Set the fried, nutty crumbs to one side.
- Peel and finely chop the onion.
- In a large pan cook the onions in a little oil until soft but not coloured. Meanwhile roughly chop the mushrooms.
- Open the tinned tomatoes and chop them. (I use scissors for this job, holding the can in my left hand and using the scissors with my right.)
- To the cooked onion add the chopped mushrooms, oregano, and the chopped tomatoes. Season with salt and black pepper.
- Simmer for 15 to 20 minutes.
- Pour the cooked tomatoes and mushrooms into an ovenproof dish and top with the nutty crumbs.
- Bake for 30 to 40 minutes. After 20 minutes investigate and cover with foil if the nutty crumbs are colouring too much.
- Serve with jacket potatoes and a couple of nice salads.

Nutty Mushrooms!

VEGGIE, VEGAN & FISH

SMOKED SALMON
SPINACH & GRAPE ROULADE

It's green, it looks spectacular, it can be made well in advance and it's truly delicious!

PREHEAT OVEN: 180°C or 350°F or GAS 4
SILICON PAPER LINED SWISS ROLL TIN

2 ozs butter	fresh nutmeg & black pepper
2 ozs plain flour	5 ozs smoked salmon slivers
1 pint milk	1/2 pint double cream
3 bayleaves	2 ozs cream cheese
6 ozs spinach	juice of 1/2 lemon
4 eggs separated	1/2 lb seedless grapes
5 ozs mature cheddar cheese	

- In a pan melt the butter. Add the flour. Cook for 2 minutes.
- Whilst stirring, gradually add the milk until the sauce boils, thickens and is very smooth. Pop the bayleaves into the sauce and simmer for 2 more minutes. Remove from the heat.
- Allow to cool for half an hour. Remove the bayleaves.
- Meanwhile wash the spinach and remove any fibrous stalks.
- Pour boiling hot water over the spinach and drain thoroughly.
- Whiz the spinach in a food processor until chopped small.
- Beat the egg yolks, cheese and spinach into the cooled sauce.
- Season with lots of freshly grated nutmeg and black pepper.
- Whisk the egg whites until stiff. <u>Gently</u> fold into the sauce.
- Pour the mixture into the lined tin and spread out evenly.
- Bake for about 30 to 40 minutes until firm but not dry.
- When cooked, cool in the tin and then turn out on to another sheet of silicon paper. Carefully peel off the old paper.
- For the filling, softly whip the cream and the cream cheese.
- Add the lemon juice to taste. Spread evenly over the roulade and strew with lots of grapes and the smoked salmon slivers.
- Using the paper to help you, carefully roll up the roulade.
- Transfer to a platter and decorate with grapes and greenery.

VEGGIE, VEGAN & FISH

PINE NUT PARCEL SERVED ON A BED OF FARMHOUSE RATATOUILLE

This recipe uses Farmhouse Puff Pastry from the 'Back to Basics' chapter. In order to qualify as a possible vegan dish, substitute vegan margarine for the butter.

PREHEAT OVEN: 200°C or 400°F or GAS 6

1 large onion
3 tablespoons olive oil
4 ozs pine nuts
3 ozs breadcrumbs
1 teaspoon dried thyme
½ tablespoon lemon juice
generous gratings of nutmeg
salt and black pepper
½ recipe quantity Farmhouse Puff Pastry (see index)

- Peel and chop the onion. Sweat in the olive oil for 5 minutes.
- Tip the oily onions into a bowl and add the pine nuts, breadcrumbs, thyme, lemon juice, nutmeg, salt and pepper.
- Stir thoroughly to mix the parcel stuffing.
- Roll out the pastry to form a 14 x 8 inch rectangle.
- Spoon the stuffing mixture into a long line down the centre of the pastry.
- Dampen the pastry edges then neatly fold the two short ends over the stuffing, followed by the two longer sides.
- <u>Carefully</u> turn the parcel over on to a greased baking sheet placing the untidy joins underneath.
- Using a pair of scissors, snip one straight line of decorative steam holes along the full length of the parcel.
- Bake for 30 to 40 minutes until the pastry is cooked. Half way through, brush the top of the pastry with some of the oil that has oozed from the parcel.
- Serve on a bed of Farmhouse Ratatouille (see index) but please don't forget to substitute olive oil for the butter if you're cooking a vegan meal.

What's in Your Parcel?

MUSHROOM, CREAM, TARRAGON & CIDER STUFFED CREPES

For the crepe filling see index for mushroom, cream, tarragon & cider soup recipe.

4 oz plain flour
1 teaspoon tarragon
1/2 teaspoon salt
1 egg
1/2 to 3/4 pint milk
1 tablespoon oil or melted butter

- Put the flour, tarragon and salt into a large bowl. Mix in the eggs then gradually beat in the milk. The batter should be the consistency of very thin cream, so adjust the milk accordingly. Beat until really smooth. (I do this in a food processor).
- Brush an omelette pan with a little oil or melted butter and set the pan on to a high heat.
- When the pan starts to smoke hot, pour in two to three tablespoons of batter, tipping the pan as you pour it in so that the mixture thinly and evenly coats the pan.
- Cook for about a minute until the crepe is set on top and golden brown underneath.
- Flip the crepe over to cook the other side.
- When cooked transfer to a wire rack to cool.
- Make as many crepes as required, allowing one per person.
- Assemble the crepes 15 minutes before you want to serve.
- Bring the mushroom, tarragon and cider soup to the boil.
- Using a slotted spoon strain some of the bulk from the soup and fill each crepe.
- I always fill and roll up the crepes on the serving platter, as they are very difficult to move once filled.
- Keep the crepes hot until you are ready to serve.
- <u>Just before</u> bringing to the table pour a little of the hot mushroom and cider soupy sauce over the platter of crepes.

MEDLEY OF FISH PIE

This is so called because any white fish at all is suitable. I tend to use haddock for the first 1/2 lb of white fish and thereafter make up the rest with any other fish available. This tasty dish is bland to the eye so serve with plenty of <u>colourful</u> vegetables and salads.

PREHEAT OVEN: 190°C or 375°F or GAS 5

2 onions
1½ lbs potatoes
1½ lbs white fish fillets
½ lb smoked haddock fillet
2 tablespoons white wine
3 bayleaves
4 ozs button mushrooms
4 ozs mature cheddar cheese
3 ozs butter
2 tablespoons plain flour
¼ pint double cream
small bunch parsley
fresh nutmeg
4 ozs prawns (optional)
3 hard boiled eggs

- Peel and chop the onions. Par boil the potatoes. Drain and cool.
- Place the fish, wine, bayleaves and ½ the onions in a pan.
- Barely cover with water and bring slowly to the boil. Simmer for 5 minutes. Drain off the resulting stock and reserve ½ pint.
- Flake the fish. Discard any skin. Allow the flaked fish to cool.
- Chop the mushrooms. Grate the cheese. Put both to one side.
- To make the sauce, melt 2 ozs of the butter, add the rest of chopped onion and gently cook until soft but not coloured.
- Sprinkle on the flour and thoroughly stir to mix well.
- Blend in the reserved fish stock. Stirring, bring to the boil.
- Add the cheese, mushrooms, cream, scissor-chopped parsley and several gratings of fresh nutmeg. Cook for 2 to 3 minutes.
- Put the flaked fish, prawns and shelled, chopped, boiled eggs in a pie dish. Pour the cheesy mushroom sauce over the top.
- Slice the par-boiled potatoes. Arrange in overlapping layers on top of the fish. Brush the top of potatoes with melted butter.
- Bake for 30 to 40 minutes until bubbling and golden brown.

VEGGIE, VEGAN & FISH

FENNEL TROUT SERVED WITH A LEMON CREAM SAUCE

1 whole cleaned trout per person
1 'feather' of herb fennel per trout
½ oz butter per trout
juice of ½ lemon per trout
½ pint double cream
juice of 1 lemon

- With a very sharp knife remove the head and tail from each trout. Thoroughly wash the trout inside and out.
- Pop a 'feather' of herb fennel, the butter and finally the lemon juice into the clean belly cavity of each trout.
- Cooking no more than 2 at a time lay the trout on a large plate suitable for the microwave. Cover with another upturned plate.
- Cook in the microwave on full power for 5 minutes. Rest the trout for 5 minutes. Cook again on full power for 5 minutes.
- <u>Cooking note:</u> It is imposssible to be specific about the length of cooking time as each trout, and each microwave is different. To test if the trout is cooked, use your thumb and forefinger and try to ease the backbone fin out of the fish. If the trout is cooked the fin and the skin will tidily peel from the flesh of the fish. If the fin and skin are difficult to remove, cook again for another couple of minutes.
- While the trout is cooking make the lemon cream sauce.
- Pour the double cream into a saucepan and bring to the boil.
- Lower the heat and add the lemon juice. Stir well.
- Keep the sauce warm until ready to serve. Do not boil again.
- With the aid of a couple of fishslices or spatulas, transfer the trout to a serving platter.
- Carefully and tidily peel the skin off the uppermost side of each fish removing the backbone fin at the same time.
- Decorate with a fennel 'feather' and lemon wedges.
- Let your guests help themselves to lemon cream sauce.

Make Sure you Read the 'Cooking Note' Before You Start!

'NEW FARM'
BACK TO BASICS

On reading the previous pages you could possibly be led to believe that I am a 'foodie purist'. This is most definitely not so. I am a farmer's wife who enjoys good food and although I take the greatest pleasure in making, growing or rearing most of the food that I serve, of course I cheat, albeit only a wee bit! I can't be cheating that much because on the very rare occasions that I buy 'sliced bread' my children think it is a huge treat! Almost everything in this 'Back to Basics' chapter can be bought in your local supermarket but I prefer to make my own.

However, one or two pre-prepared foods creep into my pantry at certain times of the year. Listed below are the ones I feel guilty about for not always making or growing myself. I make no excuses other than I actually like them either for their convenience when I'm extra busy in the summer or for their taste in a particular dish, or in some cases, for both reasons.

Tinned plum tomatoes – a useful standby soup and sauce ingredient.
Tinned pears & apricots – in some recipes, better than fresh.
Hellmann's mayonnaise – Shock! Horror! I like it.
Heinz salad cream – Shock! Horror! I like this too.
Frozen peas & green beans – I can't grow them in any quantity.
Vegetable and chicken stock cubes – quick and ready to use.
Cartons of natural yoghurt – when I need it in a rush.

Well the truth is out! I don't always have enough time to make my own mayonnaise, yoghurt or stock, so I find the commercial equivalents do have a space in my pantry. (I hope real 'foodie purists' will forgive me.) I console my guilt with the fact that I never, nor will I ever, buy ready-made, microwaveable meals!

For Convenience, Please Forgive Me!

'NEW FARM' BACK TO BASICS

MY DAILY BREAD

NUTTY BREAD

QUICK SODA BREAD

SHORTCRUST PASTRY

FARMHOUSE PUFF PASTRY

SAVOURY ONION SCONES

FARMHOUSE VINAIGRETTE

'NEW FARM' MAYONNAISE

YOGHURT & MINT MAYONNAISE DRESSING

FARMHOUSE YOGHURT

MY DAILY BREAD

To make the dough takes 7 minutes from start to finish with a Kenwood food mixer. If you haven't got a food mixer don't panic! Mix and knead the dough by hand. If you haven't got any loaf tins use cake tins. To make a rather nice looking cottage loaf, place a round of dough in the bottom of a cake tin, place another smaller round on top, then poke your finger down through the middle almost to the bottom round. Prove and bake in the usual way.

3¼ lbs strong white flour
2 ozs granulated sugar
½ tablespoon table salt
1 sachet easy blend dried yeast
2 pints hand-hot water

- Put the flour, sugar, salt and yeast into the Kenwood bowl.
- Using either the dough hook or the K-beater (I use the K-beater) blend for 5 seconds to mix the dry ingredients.
- Pour in all the water then, with the Kenwood on minimum speed knead to make a coherent, elastic dough (better the wetter side of dry).
- Leave the Kenwood on minimum speed for about one minute.
- In the time it takes to grease your loaf tins the Kenwood mixer will have kneaded the dough well enough.
- Turn the dough out on to a well-floured work surface.
- Cut into 3 even-sized pieces and knead lightly into shape.
- Place shaped dough into the tins and leave to prove (rise) in a warm place for about an hour or until the dough has doubled.
- Bake in a hot oven (200°C/400°F/Gas 6) for 30 to 40 minutes until the bottom of the loaves sounds hollow when tapped.
- Turn out on to a rack to cool.

7 Minutes from Start to Finish!

NUTTY BREAD

Making this bread is virtually identical to making 'My Daily Bread'. It is quicker if you have a Kenwood but you can just as easily mix and knead the dough by hand. Although there are no nuts in this recipe the bread has a moist nutty flavour and lots of texture from the mixed seeds.

2¼ lbs malted granary flour
1 lb strong white flour
2 ozs sugar
½ tablespoon table salt
4 tablespoons pumpkin seeds

2 tablespoons sesame seeds
3 tablespoons sunflower seeds
2 tablespoons poppy seeds
1 sachet easy blend dried yeast
2 pints hand-hot water

- Put the malted granary and the strong white flour, the sugar, salt, all four kinds of seeds and the yeast into the Kenwood.
- Using either the dough hook or the K-beater blend for 5 seconds to mix the dry ingredients.
- Pour in all the water then, with the mixer on minimum speed, knead the dough to make a coherent, elastic dough (better on the wetter side of dry).
- Leave the Kenwood on minimum speed for about one minute.
- In the time it takes to grease your loaf tins the Kenwood mixer will have kneaded the dough well enough.
- Turn the dough out on to a well-floured work surface.
- Cut into 4 even sized pieces and knead lightly into shape.
- Place the dough into the tins and leave to prove (rise) in a warm place for about an hour or until the dough has doubled.
- Bake in a hot oven (200°C/400°F/Gas 6) for 30 to 40 minutes until the bottom of the loaves sounds hollow when tapped.
- Turn out on to a wire rack to cool.

Nice and Nutty!

BACK TO BASICS

QUICK SODA BREAD

If I haven't got time to wait for my 'daily bread' to rise then I make soda bread. It's very quick to mix the dough, it only requires gentle kneading and it's baked immediately. The only problem with it is that it has no keeping qualities but that doesn't matter because it will be eaten up quickly anyway!

1 lb plain white flour
1 level teaspoon bicarbonate of soda
1 level teaspoon cream of tartar
1 heaped tablespoon caster sugar
a pinch of salt
3/4 pint milk

OVEN TEMP: 220°C or 425°F or GAS 7

- In a large bowl thoroughly mix the flour, bicarbonate of soda, cream of tartar, sugar and salt.
- Make a well in the centre and pour in the milk.
- Using a wooden spoon mix in the milk until a soft, very wet dough is formed.
- Turn/pour the dough on to a well-floured worktop.
- Sprinkle the top of the wet dough with flour and knead lightly.
- Shape into a round and place in a well-greased, loose-bottomed cake tin.
- With a knife lightly score the top of the dough into 8 even-sized portions.
- Bake in the oven for 20 minutes.
- Reduce the heat to 180°C or 350°F or GAS 4 and cook for a further 20 to 30 minutes.
- If the bread sounds hollow when tapped on the bottom, it's cooked. Cool on a wire rack but serve whilst still warm.

Eaten as Quickly as it's Made!

SHORTCRUST PASTRY

8 ozs plain flour
1/2 teaspoon salt
2 ozs lard
2 ozs butter
2 tablespoons cold water to mix

- Mix together the flour and salt in a bowl.
- Rub the lard and butter into the dry ingredients until the mixture resembles fine breadcrumbs.
- Sprinkle water over the crumbs and mix together to form a soft, firm dough.
- Press the mixture together with your fingertips handling carefully. It should leave the sides of the bowl and the fingertips quite clean.
- Cover and chill for at least half an hour (if you have time).
- Roll out and use as required.

FARMHOUSE PUFF PASTRY

8 ozs plain flour
1/2 teaspoon salt
8 ozs butter
1 teaspoon lemon juice
1/4 pint cold water

- In a large bowl mix together the flour and salt.
- Cut the butter into walnut sized pieces and add to the flour.
- Mix the lemon juice and water together and add to the bowl.
- Mix to form a soft dough, keeping the pieces of butter whole.
- Roll into a rectangle and fold in three, envelope style.
- Seal the open edges by pressing with the rolling pin.
- Give the pastry a 1/4 turn to the left.
- Roll, fold and turn three more times.
- Chill for at least an hour (if you have time).
- Roll out and use as required.

SAVOURY ONION SCONES

*I have adapted this from a recipe in an excellent book that has become totally indispensable to me. It is called **Through My Kitchen Window** and was written by the famous, award-winning Irish cookery writer, **Margaret Browne**. Thank you Margaret, you have been a great encouragement to me in the writing of my recipe books. Margaret also runs a similar establishment to myself, called **Ballymakeigh House, Killeagh, County Cork, Ireland**. Ballymakeigh is a lot more upmarket than 'New Farm' but we all need somebody to aspire to don't we!*

OVEN TEMP: 400°F or 200°C or GAS 6

1 lb finely chopped onions
6 ozs butter
1 tablespoon olive oil
1 lb plain flour
2 teaspoons caraway seeds
3 teaspoons baking powder
2 ozs caster sugar
2 tblsps medium curry powder
3 ozs mature cheddar cheese
a little milk to mix

- Gently cook the onions in 2 ozs of the butter and all the oil until well cooked but not coloured. Allow to cool completely.
- In a large bowl mix the flour, caraway seeds, baking powder, sugar and curry powder. Rub in the remaining butter and the grated cheese.
- Add the cooled onions and enough milk to bring the mixture together to form a soft, moist dough.
- Turn the dough out on to a well-floured worktop. Gently roll out to about $1^1/_2$ inches thick and cut into rounds.
- Place on a floured baking sheet and bake in the oven for 15 to 20 minutes and, as Margaret Browne suggests in her book, half way through the baking turn the scones, as they tend to burn underneath.

A Savoury Scone Sensation!

FARMHOUSE VINAIGRETTE

This dressing works well on all sorts of salads but I use it mostly on barley & apricot salad and on sliced, ripe tomatoes.

½ pint good olive oil
¼ pint malt vinegar
2 cloves garlic
1 tablespoon chopped fresh herbs
2 heaped teaspoons whole grain mustard
2 teaspoons honey
salt and black pepper

- Pour the olive oil and malt vinegar into a large, screw-top jar.
- Peel and finely chop the garlic cloves.
- Wash and chop a selection of fresh herbs, e.g. basil, oregano, thyme and mint.
- Add the garlic, herbs, mustard, sugar, salt and pepper to the jar. Put the lid on and shake well.
- Taste and adjust the seasoning.

'NEW FARM' MAYONNAISE

2 whole eggs
½ level teaspoon dry English mustard
a pinch of salt
½ teaspoon caster sugar
4 tablespoons white wine vinegar
½ pint vegetable oil

- Place all the ingredients, except the oil, into a liquidizer.
- Turn on to blend and <u>slowly</u> drizzle the oil through the hole in the top of the lid.
- Continue to blend and the mayonnaise will gradually thicken up.

Get Your Salad Dressed!

BACK TO BASICS

YOGHURT & MINT MAYONNAISE DRESSING

When I'm out for a walk on New Farm Moor, I gather wild mint growing by the side of the burns (Scottish word for streams). However, when in a hurry, and walking is the last thing on my mind, I send one of the children out to the herb garden for some applemint!

natural yoghurt (see index)
'Hellmann's' mayonnaise
fresh mint

- In a large screw-top jar combine equal quantities of natural yoghurt and 'Hellmann's' mayonnaise. (It really doesn't work with homemade mayonnaise – I've tried it!)
- Add a generous handful of fresh, scissor-chopped mint and shake to mix well.
- Refrigerate for at least an hour to allow the mint to infuse.
- This keeps well in the fridge for several days.

How do I use this versatile dressing?

I drizzle it over soups and starters.
I use it on a stand-alone basis on the 'grazing' buffet table.
I pour it over chopped cucumber as a salad, topped with poppy seeds.
I pour it over hard-boiled eggs & serve with nutty bread as a starter.
I serve it on the side with 'Loch Fad' trout or cold meat.
Ever heard of minced beef and yoghurt plate pie? DDDDelicious ..!

Whichever way I use it I always use another little sprig of mint to decorate the finished dish. It's so useful that I usually have a good quantity ready and waiting in the fridge.

A Versatile Dressing!

FARMHOUSE YOGHURT

Most people serve their yoghurt cold but hot yoghurt for breakfast is delicious. I usually serve it with 'orange porridge' but that's another recipe for another day!

2 tblsps natural yoghurt (buy a small pot)
2 tblsps dried milk powder
1 pint full cream milk

- In a bowl, cream the natural yoghurt and the powdered milk together with a little of the fresh milk to single cream consistency.
- Bring the rest of the fresh milk to the boil and simmer for about 5 minutes. (This gives you thicker yoghurt.)
- Remove from the heat and allow to cool to about 'blood' heat. (Test with a clean finger.)
- Pour the warm milk on to the creamed yoghurt and powdered milk mixture and mix well.
- Cover and put in a warm place for at least 12 hours.
- Investigate at intervals after 4 hours.
- When the yoghurt has thickened it is ready to serve.
- It is best made fresh on a daily basis but it will keep for a few days in the fridge.

When I make yoghurt I put it on the back of the AGA. However, it can be made in a yoghurt maker, a vacuum flask or you could put it in a covered bowl, insulated with a thick towel in any warm place. To make a soft cheese, transfer the set yoghurt to a muslin or jelly bag and leave to drip overnight. You can flavour the resulting cheese with either savoury or sweet. For savoury cheese maybe add some finely chopped garlic and/or fresh scissor-chopped herbs. For a sweet cheese use your imagination with a little honey, figs, or apricots.

Eat with a Clear Conscience and Feel Healthy!

'NEW FARM'

A WEE TASTE BUD TICKLER!

This chapter is designed as a 'wee taste bud tickler' for

THE 'NEW FARM' SWEETS RECIPE BOOK.

This second and next book in the series is written and illustrated in the same farmhouse style and is full of recipes for desserts, hot puddings, ice creams, sorbets, after-dinner sweeties, cakes and all things truly delicious to eat.

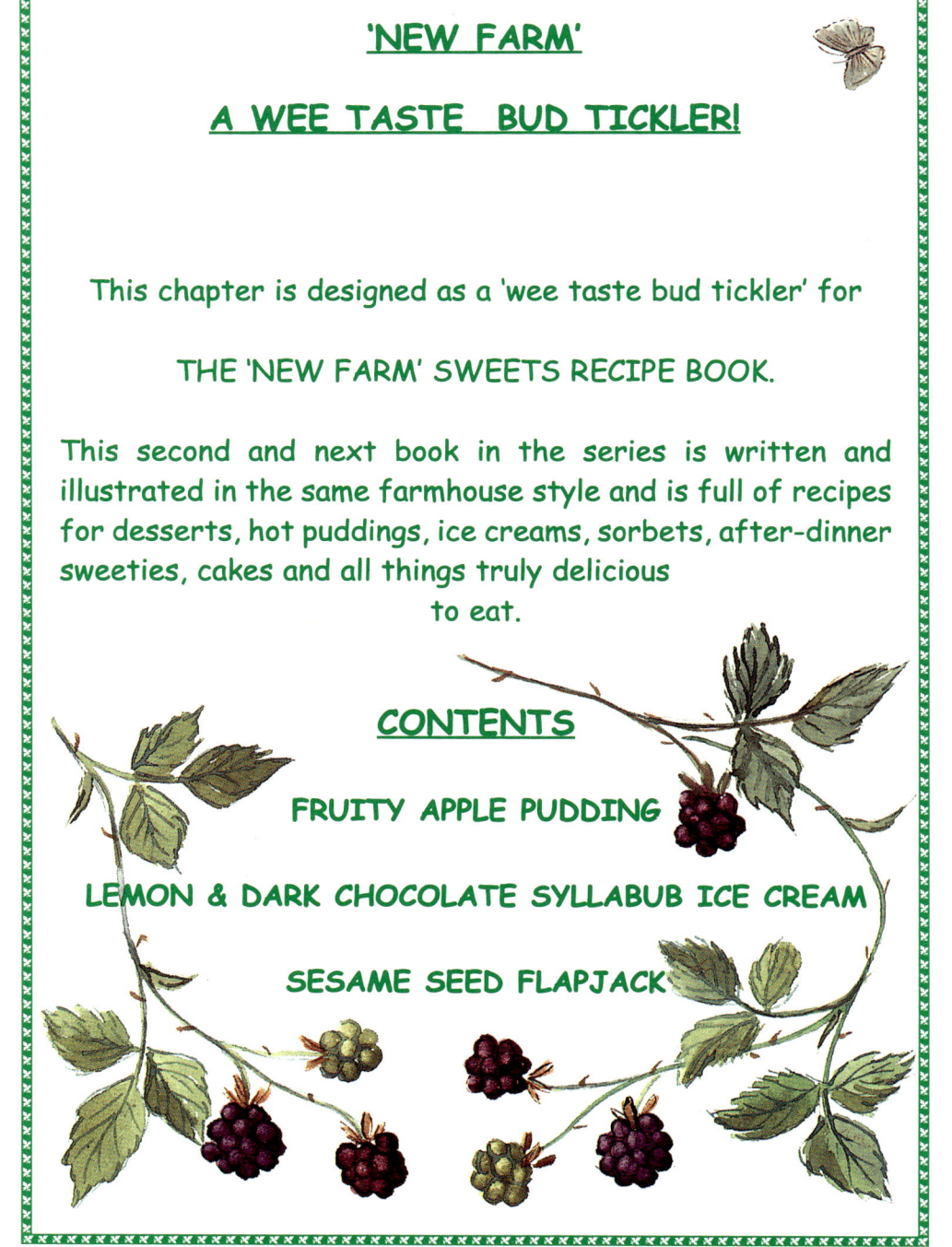

CONTENTS

FRUITY APPLE PUDDING

LEMON & DARK CHOCOLATE SYLLABUB ICE CREAM

SESAME SEED FLAPJACK

A WEE TASTE BUD TICKLER! – PUDDINGS

FRUITY APPLE PUDDING

Served hot this is a great winter warming pud.
Or serve it cold as a tasty teatime treat.

PREHEAT OVEN: 190°C or 375°F or GAS 5
GREASED 12 x 10 inch shallow cake tin

8 ozs butter	rind & juice of a lemon
8 ozs light muscovado sugar	4 tablespoons mincemeat
1 lb self-raising flour	2 ozs demerara sugar
2 eggs	1 teaspoon cinnamon
1 lb cooking apples	1 oz porridge oats

icing sugar for dredging

- Slowly melt the butter in a saucepan.
- Add the muscovado sugar and stir well to dissolve. Take off the heat to cool slightly.
- Put the flour into a large bowl. Add melted butter and sugar.
- Beat the eggs and add to the mixture, stirring well to combine.
- Transfer two-thirds of the base mixture to the cake tin.
- Peel, slice and cook the apples. (Use your microwave.)
- Place the cooked apples in a large bowl with the rind and juice of the lemon, mincemeat, demerara sugar and cinnamon.
- Mix well then spoon the 'applely mincemeat' over the base of the tin in an even layer.
- Mix the porridge oats into the leftover base mixture and scatter/spread evenly over the 'applely mincemeat' layer.
- Bake in the oven for about 30 to 40 minutes.
- Serve hot or cold dredged with icing sugar, accompanied with pouring cream or homemade vanilla custard.

Serve Hot as a Pud, or Cold as a Cake!

A WEE TASTE BUD TICKLER! – ICE CREAMS

LEMON & DARK CHOCOLATE SYLLABUB ICE CREAM

Ideal after a rich, meaty meal or serve as an easy dessert for a light-hearted lunch.
With the leftover egg yolks why not make some lemon curd.

4 egg whites
8 ozs caster sugar
Juice of 1 lemon
¼ pint medium white wine
1 pint double cream
2 ozs dark cooking chocolate

- Whisk the egg whites until stiff but not dry.
- Whip the double cream to soft peak stage (not buttery).
- Gently fold the sugar, lemon juice, wine and whipped double cream into the egg whites.
- Coarsely grate the dark chocolate.
- Fold the chocolate evenly into the ice cream.
- Pour into any shape of mould and freeze for at least 24 hours.

You can serve direct from your freezer. If you freeze in a terrine dish, it slices really easily. Sometimes you may have to flash dip the mould in very hot water but only for 3 or 4 seconds.
It is really decadent served with more double cream poured over.
Don't forget to use the herbs and flowers from the garden to decorate the finished dish. It really will taste even nicer if it looks good! Serve with fresh fruit such as strawberries or raspberries.

Forget the Calories...
Just Eat, Savour and Enjoy!

SESAME SEED FLAPJACK

This is a great stand-by to have in the cake tin. (If you can get it to last long enough to make it to the cake tin!) I often serve this at breakfast time (cut into 2 inch squares) and re-name it Cereal Cake, or, I cut it a lot, lot smaller to serve with coffee as an after-dinner sweetie.

PREHEAT OVEN: 190°C or 375°F or GAS 5
GREASED 12 x 10 inch shallow baking tray

8 ozs butter
2 tablespoons golden syrup
4 ozs porridge oats
4 ozs self-raising flour
8 ozs soft brown sugar
6 ozs <u>crushed</u> cornflakes
3 tablespoons sesame seeds
cold running water

- Melt the butter and golden syrup (I use my microwave).
- Take off the heat to cool slightly and transfer to a large bowl.
- Add the oats, flour, sugar, <u>crushed</u> cornflakes and sesame seeds. Stir well to mix together evenly.
- Butter the baking tray and spread the mixture about ¾ inch thick. (If there is any leftover mixture, cook it in another smaller tray or on a buttered, ovenproof plate.)
- With the tap running, wet your hand. Pat and press down on the mixture until the top is smooth and there is a <u>slight</u> film of water on the flapjack.
- Bake in the oven for <u>no more</u> than 10 to 15 minutes. Watch carefully because it will catch and burn really quickly. It should hardly colour at all and still be quite soft.
- Cool slightly, cut into squares and leave till cold in the tray.

Made with clear, runny honey instead of golden syrup this flapjack has a completely different flavour. Try it, and see for yourself!

Chewy, Sticky & Very, Very Moreish!

'NEW FARM'

WEIGHING OF INGREDIENTS

My farmhouse style of cooking does <u>not</u> require precise weighing of ingredients so don't worry whether you measure in imperial or metric. All the recipes in this book use imperial measurements but if you prefer to use metric then go for it! You may find the chart below provides a useful guide.

Imperial	Metric
2 tablespoons	20 mls
4 tablespoons	40 mls
¼ pint	150 mls
½ pint	300 mls
1 pint	600 mls
½ oz	15 grams
1 oz	30 grams
2 ozs	60 grams
4 ozs	120 grams
8 ozs	240 grams
1 lb	480 grams

All the recipes in this book are regularly cooked in my farmhouse kitchen using <u>Imperial Measurements</u>.

FOR YOU OWN RECIPE NOTES

INDEX

AGA Style Potatoes	39	Beetroot Vinaigrette Mould	28
Apple		**Braised Red Cabbage with…**	42
Apple, Mint & Melon Salad	33	**Bread**	
Crisp Apple & Ginger Salad	29	My Daily Bread	70
Fruity Apple Pudding	79	Nutty Bread	71
Sausagemeat Sage & Sweet Apple Pie	55	Quick Soda Bread	72
Apricot		**Broccoli**	
Apricot & Scallion Loaf	60	Stilton & Broccoli Bake	61
Barley Apricot & Mint Vinaigrette	28	**Broths**	
Pork Casseroled with Apricots	49	Barley Broth with Carrots …	20
Aubergines		Potato & Bayleaf Broth	18
'Woodend' Aubergines	41	Smoked Haddock & Fennel Broth	16
		Brown Ale	
Back to Basics	69	Beef Braised in…	52
Farmhouse Puff Pastry	73	**Bulb Fennel**	
Farmhouse Vinaigrette	75	Bulb Fennel & Cucumber Soup	23
Farmhouse Yoghurt	77		
My Daily Bread	70	**Cabbage**	
'New Farm' Mayonnaise	75	Braised Red Cabbage with Crab Apple	42
Nutty Bread	71	Caraway Cabbage	43
Quick Soda Bread	72	Pineapple & Pumpkin Seed Coleslaw	30
Savoury Onion Scones	74	**Cakes**	
Shortcrust Pastry	73	Sesame Seed Flapjack	81
Yoghurt & Mint Mayonnaise Dressing	76	**Caraway**	
Barley		Caraway Cabbage	43
Barley, Apricot & Mint Vinaigrette	28	Carrot & Caraway Seed Salad	30
Barley Broth with Carrots & Cream	20	Carrot & Caraway Soup	17
Beef Braised in Brown Ale with…	52	Carrots & Caraway	45
Lamb Casseroled with Plum Tomatoes	48	**Carrots**	
Basil		Beetroot, Carrot & Courgette Salad	29
Beef Braised in Brown Ale with…	52	Carrot & Caraway Soup	17
Lamb Casseroled with Plum Tomatoes	48	Carrot Orange & Fresh Mint Soup	15
Tomato & Basil Soup	19	Carrot & Caraway Seed Salad	30
Batter		Carrots & Caraway	45
Beef Braised in Brown Ale with	52	Carrot Salad	32
Bayleaf		**Casseroles**	
Potato & Bayleaf Soup	18	Beef Braised in Brown Ale with…	52
Beans		Lamb Casseroled with Plum Tomatoes	48
Green Beans & Garlic	43	Pork Casseroled with Apricots	49
Beef		**Cauliflower**	
Beef Braised in Brown Ale with…	52	Cream of Cauliflower & Cheddar Soup	22
Beetroot		Crunchy Cauliflower Salad	27
Beetroot, Carrot & Courgette Salad	29		

Cheese
Cream of Cauliflower & Cheddar Soup	22
Isle of Bute Cheddar Cheese	22
Stilton & Broccoli Bake	61
Chicken: **Cherried Duck & Orange**	50

Chocolate
Lemon & Dark Chocolate Ice Cream	80

Cider
Mushroom Tarragon & Cider Soup	21
Mushroom Tarragon & Cider Crepes	65

Coleslaw
30

Courgette
Beetroot Carrot & Courgette Salad	29

Crab Apple Jelly
Braised Red Cabbage with……	42

Cream
Barley Broth with Carrots & Cream	20
Cream of Cauliflower Soup	22
Lemon Cream Sauce	67
Mushroom Cream Tarragon Soup	21
Mushroom Cream & Cider Crepes	65

Crepes
Mushroom Cream Tarragon & Cider	65

Crumble
Mushroom & Oregano Crumble	62

Cucumber
Bulb Fennel & Cucumber Soup	23

Curly Kale & Ginger Butter
38

Desserts
Fruity Apple Pudding	79
Lemon & Dark Chocolate Ice Cream	80
Sesame Seed Flapjack	81

Dressings
Farmhouse Vinaigrette	75
'New Farm' Mayonnaise	75
Yoghurt & Mint Mayonnaise Dressing	76

Duck
Cherried Duck with Orange	50

Dumplings
Tarragon Dumplings	49

Farmhouse
Farmhouse Puff Pastry	73
Farmhouse Ratatouille	37
Farmhouse Vinaigrette	75
Farmhouse Yoghurt	77

Fennel
Bulb Fennel & Cucumber Soup	23
Fennel Potatoes	44
Fennel Trout with a Lemon Sauce	67
Smoked Haddock & Fennel Soup	16

Fish
Fennel Trout & Lemon Cream Sauce	67
Medley of Fish Pie	66
Smoked Haddock & Fennel Soup	16

Flapjack
Sesame Seed Flapjack	81

Garlic
Green Beans & Garlic	43
Wild Garlic Potatoes	44

Ginger
Crisp Apple & Ginger Salad	29
Curly Kale & Ginger Butter	38

Grapes
Smoked Salmon & Grape Roulade	63

Green Beans
Green Beans and Garlic	43

Haddock, Smoked
Smoked Haddock & Fennel Soup	16

Ham
Ham & Pineapple Pudding	57

Ice Cream
Lemon & Dark Chocolate Ice Cream	80

Isle of Bute
Isle of Bute Mature Cheddar Cheese	22

Lamb
Lamb Casseroled with Plum Tomatoes	48
Lemon & Thyme Stuffed Lamb	54

Leek
Leek & Potato Mash	36
Leek & Potato Soup	14

Lemon
Lemon Cream Sauce	67
Lemon & Dark Chocolate Ice Cream	80
Lemon & Thyme Stuffed Lamb	54

Mash
Leek & Potato Mash	36

Mayonnaise
	75
'New Farm' Mayonnaise	75
Yoghurt & Mint Mayonnaise Dressing	76

Meaty Main Courses
	47
Beef Braised in Brown Ale with...	52
Cherried Duck with Orange	50
Ham & Pineapple Pudding	57
Lamb Casseroled with Plum Tomatoes	48
Lemon & Thyme Stuffed Lamb	54
Peppered Pork & Potato Pie	56
Pork Casseroled with Apricots and...	49
Sausage & Apple Parcels	51
Sausagemeat Sage & Sweet Apple...	55
Sweet & Sour Belly Pork Ribs	53

Melon
Apple Mint & Melon Salad	33

Mint
Apple Mint & Melon Salad	33
Barley Apricot & Mint Vinaigrette	28
Carrot Orange & Fresh Mint Soup	15

Mother's Wet Salad
	31

Mushrooms
Mushroom Cream Tarragon Soup	21
Mushroom Cream Tarragon Crepes	65
Mushroom & Oregano Crumble	62

Natural Yoghurt
	77
Farmhouse Yoghurt	77

Onion
Savoury Onion Scones	74

Orange
Carrot Orange & Fresh Mint Soup	15

Cherried Duck with Orange	50

Oregano
Mushroom & Oregano Crumble	62

Parsnips
Roasted Parsnips	40

Pastry
Farmhouse Puff Pastry	73
Shortcrust Pastry	73

Pies
Medley of Fish Pie	66
Peppered Pork & Potato Pie	56
Sausagemeat Sage & Sweet Apple Pie	55

Pineapple
Ham & Pineapple Pudding	57
Pineapple & Pumpkin Seed Coleslaw	30

Pine Nuts
Pine Nut Parcel Served on a ...	64

Pork
Peppered Pork & Potato Pie	56
Pork Casseroled with Apricots and...	49
Sweet & Sour Belly Pork Ribs	53

Potato
AGA Style Potatoes	39
Fennel Potatoes	44
Hot Potato & Thyme Salad	26
Leek & Potato Mash	36
Leek & Potato Soup	14
Peppered Pork & Potato Pie	56
Potato & Bayleaf Soup	18
Wild Garlic Potatoes	44

Puddings – Savoury
Basil Batter Puddings	52
Ham & Pineapple Pudding	57

Puddings – Sweet
Fruity Apple Pudding	79
Lemon & Dark Chocolate Ice Cream	80
Sesame Seed Flapjack	81

Puff Pastry
	73

Pumpkin Seed
Nutty Bread	71
Pineapple & Pumpkin Seed Coleslaw	30

PAGE 86

Ratatouille	37	**Spinach**	
Pine Nut Parcel Served on a bed of...	64	Smoked Salmon & Spinach Roulade	63
Roulade		**Stilton and Broccoli Bake**	61
Smoked Salmon & Grape Roulade	63		
		Tomato	
Sage		Tomato & Basil Soup & Sauce	19
Sausagemeat Sage & Sweet Apple Pie	55	Tossed Tomato Vinaigrette	32
Salads	25	Lamb Casseroled with Plum Tomatoes	48
Apple Mint & Melon	33	**Trout**	
Barley Apricot & Mint Vinaigrette	28	Fennel Trout Served with Lemon...	67
Beetroot Carrot & Courgette	29		
Beetroot Vinaigrette Mould	28	**Vegetables**	35
Carrot & Caraway Seed	30	AGA Style Potatoes	39
Carrot Salad	32	Braised Red Cabbage with...	42
Crisp Apple & Ginger	29	Caraway Cabbage	43
Crunchy Cauliflower	27	Carrots & Caraway	45
Hot Potato & Fresh Thyme	26	Curly Kale & Ginger Butter	38
Mother's Wet Salad	31	Farmhouse Ratatouille	37
Pineapple & Pumpkin Seed Coleslaw	30	Fennel Potatoes	44
Tossed Tomato Vinaigrette	32	Green Beans & Garlic	43
Sauces		Leek & Potato Mash	36
Lemon Cream Sauce	67	Roasted Parsnips	40
Mushroom Cream Tarragon & Cider	21	Wild Garlic Potatoes	44
Tomato & Basil	19	'Woodend' Aubergines	41
Scallion		**Veggie, Vegan & Fish**	59
Apricot & Scallion Loaf	60	Apricot & Scallion Loaf	60
Scones		Fennel Trout & Lemon Cream Sauce	67
Savoury Onion Scones	74	Medley of Fish Pie	66
Sesame Seed Flapjack	81	Mushroom Cream Tarragon Crepes	65
Shortcrust Pastry	73	Mushroom & Oregano Crumble	62
Smoked Haddock & Fennel Soup	16	Pine Nut Parcel served on...	64
Smoked Salmon and......Roulade	63	Smoked Salmon & Spinach Roulade	63
Soups & Broths	13	Stilton & Broccoli Bake	61
Barley Broth with Carrots & Cream	20	**Vinaigrette**	
Bulb Fennel & Cucumber	23	Barley Apricot & Mint Vinaigrette	28
Carrot & Caraway	17	Beetroot Vinaigrette Mould	28
Carrot Orange & Fresh Mint	15	Farmhouse Vinaigrette	75
Cream of Cauliflower & Cheddar.	22	Tossed Tomato Vinaigrette	32
Leek & Potato	14		
Mushroom Cream Tarragon & Cider	21	**Wild Garlic Potatoes**	44
Potato & Bayleaf	18	**'Woodend' Aubergines**	41
Smoked Haddock & Fennel	16	**Yoghurt - Farmhouse**	77
Tomato & Basil	19	Yoghurt & Mint Mayonnaise Dressing	76

WHAT THE INSPECTORS SAY......

Every year 'New Farm' undergoes a rigorous inspection process on a 'mystery guest' basis by qualified restaurant and accommodation inspectors. The inspectors stay overnight and thoroughly assess the quality of the food, accommodation and hospitality offered. Here are some of their comments:

'TASTE OF SCOTLAND' GUIDE 1999
(The guide to the best places to eat & stay in Scotland.)

" ......Carole Howard is an accomplished baker. Her cooking is tackled with enormous enthusiasm and interest and produces imaginative and tasty meals making full use of locally sourced supplies... The views from the farmhouse are magnificent... warm welcome and homely atmosphere... interesting and convivial evening after being welcomed in Gaelic to the table."

AA 'BED & BREAKFAST' GUIDE 1999
(For the year 2000 'New Farm' has been awarded 5 diamonds, the highest possible award for a farmhouse. 'New Farm' has also been nominated for the AA's 'Dinner of the Year' award.)

"*Unique, personal, different* and *homely* are some of the words best used to describe this highly individual farmhouse...... Carole Howard has developed a dining experience that is reminiscent of farmhouse family gatherings...... Guests are seated at a communal table and help themselves to the dishes created from the farm's own produce...... many nice touches."